KYSHAW

DNA EXCHANGE

THE PAIN OF A FOSTER CHILD

Foreword by Roxane Harper

DNA EXCHANGE by Kyshawna Johnson

All scripture quotations, citing or otherwise indicated are taken from the ESV (ESV® Bible [*The Holy Bible, English Standard Version®*]); NIV (*The Holy Bible, New International Version*, NIV® Copyright © 1973, 1978, 1984, 2011 by Biblica, Inc. ®); KJV (*King James Version*, used under public domain).

Some details in stories or recollections may have been changed to protect the identities of the people or locations involved.

Hardcover ISBN: 978-1-7358959-0-1
Paperback ISBN: 978-1-7358959-1-8

Images by Ashley Byrd, A.N.S Photography, www.ansphoto.com
Cover Design by Andrew Roberson, DRU Creative Studio LLC
© 2020, www.facebook.com/drucreativestudio
Formatting & Editing by Chadash LLC, www.chadashdesign.com

Published and Printed in the United States of America.
2020 – First Edition

DNA EXCHANGE

The Pain Of A Foster Child

Dedication

To the woman who birthed me, who nurtured me, who loved me and who raised me, I dedicate this book to you, Mom, because you are the reason I am who I am today. When I wrote this book, I had you in mind. I was reminded of your strength and tenacity to fight and overcome the adversity that was thrown at you throughout your entire life. I was reminded of every time you told me to never give up, though you said it with your words. I also remember you pushing me with every hug you gave, every kiss on the forehead and every moment you sat and listened to me; and through those moments, I felt strength being transferred to me. I remember every single conversation we had about how you've been through some of the toughest situations. At that time, I didn't understand, but today I do; and that is because I, unfortunately, went through some of your similar situations.

The beauty of our story is that we fought, and we overcame what was meant to take us out. I have grown to know what strength is, what courage is, what love is and what a hero is because you were the greatest example of them all. I really miss you. And though you are not here, I will continue to carry you through my story and I will continue to let you shine through me. Thank you for instilling in me what a strong Black woman should be like because I doubt I'd be anything that I am without you and Jesus. I am proud to be your daughter; and I am proud and grateful that I was blessed to have you in my life for 13 years, Mom. Though that's not a long time, I still hold onto every memory that we shared. You were special; and because of that, I am now special. Thanks for being such an amazing mother. You were the greatest part of my life. I love and miss you, Mommy!

Foreword

Kyshawna Johnson is a delightful and anointed young woman that I had the pleasure to meet only one time. This chance meeting makes this an undeniable God Connection, especially since I have been asked to write the foreword to her book. This book, DNA Exchange, is the gritty and heart-wrenching story of her life that is full of pain, hope and purpose.

From the moment of her unexpectant entry into the world on her grandmother's kitchen floor, Kyshawna Johnson leads us on her journey of pain and betrayal. This raw, eye-opening memoir tells the story of Kyshawna's fractured childhood, the many failures of systems in place to protect children, including foster care, family and trusted adults who prey on the helpless. Her life of abuse, neglect, rejection, extreme loss and disappointment is experienced by thousands of children, including foster children in this country and around the world every day.

This book, DNA Exchange, is appropriately called, as it leads to the discovery that at times, people we trust have an insatiable desire to subvert our purpose by inputting their

DNA EXCHANGE

DNA for ours. This unnatural exchange can rob us of our God-given purpose and destiny. DNA Exchange shares how enemies of our soul attempt to change our trajectory through abuse, abandonment or just the words spoken that mold our character.

Kyshawna's struggle to overcome nearly insurmountable odds leads her to the only place of solace worth trusting: The arms of a loving God. Our true purpose is decreed by Paul in Romans, Chapter 8, where he declares that all things work together for good because we love God and are called according to His purpose. Romans 8:29: *"For those God foreknew he also predestined to be conformed to the image of his Son. . ."* (NIV). His purpose is that we be conformed to the image of Jesus Christ and not the image of man. We are being led to the realization that Jesus desires to exchange His DNA for our DNA, which is the only exchange worth living for.

John says when He appears, we will be like Him, for we shall see Him as He is. Everyone that has this hope will purify themselves and submit to the greatest DNA Exchange in the history of the world: His life for my life. *Galatians 2:20* (ESV): *"I have been crucified with Christ. It is no longer I who live, but Christ who lives in me. And the life I now live in the flesh I live by faith in the Son of God, who loved me and gave himself for me."*

- Roxane Harper

Contents

An Unexpected Birth

On a beautiful summer day, when life was going along as normally as could be expected, in the kitchen of my grandmother's home, I was born. Yes, on June 23, 1995, I made my sudden and unexpected arrival into the world! Maybe the words "sudden" and "unexpected" are catching you off guard because I am using them in relation to pregnancy and birth. Let me explain. At the time of my birth, my mother was six months pregnant with me. So, she, my four older brothers and the rest of our family *were* expecting me; but they were not expecting me to arrive in June because my mother's due date was in September. But without any further ado, I made my arrival three months early.

Unfortunately for me, though, my birth came without warning or effort, as I literally slipped from my mother's womb, and onto the kitchen floor I landed. There was no time for anyone to catch me or soften the blow. Hearing my mother's surprised screams, my grandmother (my mother's mother) came to the rescue, saw what had transpired and called the paramedics.

Gathering both my mother and me, the paramedics immediately transported us to the nearest hospital so we could receive medical attention. After being properly attended to, the time came for the doctor's diagnosis—or, rather, diagnoses of me. And to be quite frank, the diagnoses did not promise to be hopeful. First, I was diagnosed with possible brain damage due to the impact my head made with the kitchen floor. Secondly, I was addicted to drugs because my mother, who was addicted to crack cocaine and consumed the drug on a regular basis, passed the drugs in utero to me. Thirdly, it was predicted I would suffer learning disabilities and possibly health challenges. Only time would demonstrate the reality of these diagnoses.

Although my mother and I were both admitted to the hospital for medical care, a few days later, she was discharged. I, on the other hand, had to remain so I could be weaned from cocaine while also gaining the required weight. Leaving the hospital without her newborn baby, my mother was faced with a choice. She had to decide if she wanted to leave drugs in her past and care for me in the present, along with my other siblings in a drug-free environment, or remain on drugs. If she decided to remain on drugs, I would go into foster care. I am grateful to report that my mother made the choice to enter a rehabilitation program to become drug-free.

Meanwhile, I continued my hospital stay and was weaned from drugs. Once I received the doctor's clearance for release, my mother was unable to take me into her care because she was still involved with her drug treatment program. As a result, I was sent to a foster home. I remained there for a few months until my maternal grandmother came to retrieve me, taking me into her home and personal care. At that time, I had a heart monitor around my neck because I was suffering from heart complications. Thankfully, that health concern is behind me.

Once my mother finished her treatment program, I moved into her home with her and my four older brothers. At that time, we lived in a two-bedroom apartment. My mother had her room, and the other room was for my four brothers and me. However, as time progressed, my mother relapsed and returned to her drug habit. She had been fighting the battle of drug addiction for many years. Not only did she suffer from the harmful effects of drugs, all of my siblings suffered, as they were all born addicted to drugs just as I was.

Living with my mother presented several challenges for me. First of all, she was not accustomed to having a daughter after birthing four sons. Secondly, due to my mother's comfort level with me, I was usually away from home, visiting godparents, family friends or grandparents. After my mother reverted to her customary drug use, my grandmother stepped in once again and began custody paperwork for my siblings and for me. Eventually, I would move to a new residence.

Off To Grandma's

Almost every single child goes through many scenarios of separation anxiety which is caused by separation from a significant nurturant figure and typically a parent or from familiar surroundings. The first time a child will endure this level of discomfort is when they first leave the womb, being knitted to their mother for a whole nine months only to be released into a cold world filled with overwhelming sights and sounds, causing them to cry for the first time ever.

The other times these emotions will be riled up is whenever a stranger holds them, a babysitter takes care of them while the parent is gone and the first full day of school. This is not only limited to being separated from a parent, but also to just being in a different environment entirely, for you are uncertain of whether or not the present surroundings you may find yourself in are as safe and secure as the arms of those who have taken care of you. And the older you get, the more you will realize that the same way you had to come out into the cold world when you were born, that you will also have to sit in various surroundings until your temperature warms up to the change, kind of like how a cold chair or bed only gets warm once you have rested in it for an extended period of time.

I remember at the age of four years old, I would always see my mother lying on her bed sick. I mean extremely sick. I always wondered what was wrong, which I later discovered that she had Type 2 diabetes. My mother had it rough. She was raising five children all on her own while, at the same time, fighting her sickness. I recall feeling so bad for my mother because I couldn't do anything about it. The situation broke my heart seeing her lying there throwing up and looking weak.

My mother didn't want my siblings or me to see her sick, so she would have my grandmother come and get us sometimes during the week, but mainly on the weekends. All I could remember was hearing the sirens from the ambulance and fire truck arriving at my house to pick up my mother. I hated to see them coming. My mother stayed in and out of the hospital because of how bad her condition was.

There would be days and sometimes months where I wouldn't see my mother because she was in the hospital sick. I wasn't able to go see her because my mother always said, "I don't want my kids seeing me like this." So, I couldn't see her. The only thing I was able to receive was a phone call from my mother when she was well enough to speak on the phone. It did my heart well to hear her voice.

When my mother was released, she would make up the time lost and take my siblings and me out to eat or to an amusement park or arcade. It was the best time of our lives. My mother tried to stay strong emotionally, physically, mentally and spiritually for my brothers and me; but it was such a hard challenge for her. She had a rough childhood; and with all her might, she tried to prevent that from happening to me and my siblings.

She wasn't in the right state of mind to take care of me and my siblings. My mother needed support to raise me and my brothers, so she asked my grandmother to take legal custody of us because my grandmother was in a better condition. She had the living space that we would need, and it was more fun at my grandmother's house because there were more kids around the neighborhood; and my cousins would also come over.

I remember one day, my grandma came and got me,

along with my brothers from my mom's house. She told us that we were going to spend the night for a long time. Next thing I know, we never returned back to my mother. It wasn't that my mother didn't want us; she just wanted the best for us. While my mother was stable, she made sure that we were well taken care of. She fed us four times a day: Breakfast, lunch, a snack and dinner. She made sure that we were well-dressed and always well-mannered and put together. She loved her children.

And although my grandmother gained full custody of me and my siblings, my mother had always been present. She was always at my grandmother's house. The only thing that changed was our living environment. Though it wasn't the best, it was better for me, my mother and my siblings.

My grandmother started out being very caring and attentive. She did her job by taking us to our doctor's appointments, to daycare, to our therapy sessions and overall making sure that we were well.

My mother grew up amongst seven other siblings, her mother and her father. According to the conversations I had with my mother, she expressed to me that her childhood was pretty rough, growing up in poverty, facing different perversions and several forms of abuse. I learned that my story isn't that different from hers, which is something you'll later discover as you dive deeper into my story. My mother also shared that she dealt with the loss of her father, as I also did.

Finding out that me and my siblings were permanently staying with my grandmother flooded my heart with so many negative emotions. I felt as though a part of my heart was torn from my chest. The decision that was made out of my control left me feeling as though my rights to be with my mother were ripped from my life. I remember being so sad on the bus leaving from court, knowing that the night before was the last night I'd be with my mother. In my mind, I'm thinking because I am leaving my mother's house, then I must be leaving my mother permanently as well. My little mind was going through so much at the time.

I had to fight the thoughts of embarrassment and shame, you know, not living with your mother because she's a functioning drug addict, as well as being sick with diabetes. I convinced myself so much that I had a normal life; but, truthfully, I didn't. I knew what a normal life was, and mine just wasn't it. I knew what a normal life looked like, and that was to live in a household with your parents and siblings, not living with other family members.

I grew up keeping this information to myself because I knew how embarrassing it was to have parents who weren't considered normal. I grew up being afraid that I would be bullied for the decisions that my parents made. I had so many questions roaming through my mind, questions like Why me? Why did my mother and father choose these decisions? Why did they do drugs? Will my life ever go back to normal? Does my mom just not love us?

Having such questions constantly on my mind day in and day out broke my heart. But somehow, my mother knew ways of how to make me feel normal. She'd come over every single day to ensure that she was active in our lives. She would cook dinner for us, bathe us and put us in bed. I remember every single night, she would tuck me in, kiss my forehead and tell me that she loved me. And she never missed a beat. She came to us every day and made us feel complete. She made us feel hopeful that one day, things would change for her and that she would change her life.

I saw in her eyes how broken she was and how sorry she was that we had to go through such a transition. My mother wasn't a selfish individual. However, I knew there was something deeper behind her actions. So, I never once blamed her for the things she put us through. I never blamed her for the life she decided to live because she never once made us feel like she didn't want any part of our lives. She made sure she never missed a beat.

What I adored so much about my mother was that she was a strong individual. I could only imagine how hard it was to give up her kids to a system known to neglect children, a system that doesn't care about children, a system that fails kids on a daily basis. I knew that this decision was hard for her, but she knew that it was necessary for the sake of our lives and our environment.

My mother showed us so much unconditional love; and you saw it in everything that she did for us. She would keep us looking well-put together, training us to be well-mannered, well-spoken and respectful. The way she would discipline us and make sure that we were well-behaved, my mother never allowed us to get to a place in our lives that would be what the system said we would be. Foster kids are known to behave badly, be very disrespectful, spiteful and revengeful.

My mother instilled in us love and respect. She instilled in us what honor looked like and how to extend it. She showed us these things by the way she carried herself. My mother is the reason my mind changed from being embarrassed by the system to embracing where I was because she knew that someday things would work out for us.

I remember having mixed emotions about living with my grandmother because at such a young age, I desired to be around my mother. I struggled with the thoughts that if I lived with my grandmother, then I wouldn't get the chance to wake up to my mother and to be around her all the time like I desired.

Being the only girl wasn't fun. In fact, it was really boring. My brothers rarely wanted me to play with them because I was a girl and thought maybe they'd be too rough with me and they dreaded me getting hurt. That was unfortunate. And being that my mother was always sick, there was nothing that could possibly be done. All of my girl cousins were a lot older than me, and the ones that were somewhat around my age weren't at my grandma's house all the time.

So, I grew up during this time being alone a lot, begging my brothers to play with me. And I promise you they didn't like that. No, little boys don't want girls playing with their toys because, you know, maybe we'd use them the wrong way and break them or get carried away and lose them. My brothers had their share of reasons as to why they didn't want me playing with them.

Since I wasn't able to hang with my brothers, I'd find ways to entertain myself. I wasn't really an outside type of kid. I actually enjoyed being inside the house, for it felt much safer for me. I found ways to enjoy the house, like watching cartoons, playing with Barbies, coloring and watching my brothers play with their toys. I don't know what it was, but I loved watching my brothers get along as kids. They loved one another and enjoyed each other's company, and that made my heart smile. It was comforting to see them enjoy one another as they competed, play fight, built their LEGOs and played their video games.

I wasn't that much of a complicated child. All I wanted was to be around family and to feel the love. And in the moments of me watching this, it made a difference. I may not have been able to play with them, but the times I sat and watched them made it okay with me. I was grateful that I was able to live with my siblings and not be separated in the foster care system. I know stories of families being separated for unfortunate situations.

Her Ruined 3 Childhood

W hen a child is growing up, a parent or guardian's desire for that child normally is that their only concern should be eating and playing with their toys. It is a privilege if a preschooler or kindergartner is able to live in ignorant bliss and be free to dream and explore their imagination without being exposed to the dangers and despairs of life, including drugs, alcohol, violence, sexuality, terminal illness and death. Their biggest fear should normally be things like heights, water and the imaginary monsters in their closet or under the bed.

It is only a matter of time, however, when you learn that monsters are not imaginary; they do not have terrorizing appearances either. Real monsters do not have sharp claws, teeth, horns or are covered in fur. They look just like you and me. We are taught to try and see the good and purity in people from a young age. But, we are more times than not warned about the ones who have dark and twisted intentions that bring harm and danger to several people; and their own family members are not exempt from becoming victims of their darkness.

Growing up, I was not antisocial; but I preferred more to have my alone time and be by myself in my room at my grandmother's house. I have four older brothers, so it can be overwhelming being the only girl sometimes and you are in need of breaks from all the roughhousing and adrenaline. This was a normal routine for me during my childhood, but that would change suddenly at five years old on a weekend that was like none other.

While playing around with my toys, I remember a family member of mine coming inside the room late at night. She would say things like "Let's play house." At this age, I had no idea what it meant. She explained that we would be mom and dad and to act as if we had children. I thought it was strange because in my mind, I'm thinking how can two girls be a mom and dad? It was wild.

However, we continued to play. And she said, "Okay. Now is the time where we kiss each other and go to sleep." I guess, well, she kissed my lips; and I got nervous because it seemed as though she was used to this type of game and behavior. It was weird. I walked out of the room to go sit in the living room with the adults, and nobody noticed how disturbed I was as I sat there looking at everyone hoping someone would ask me what was wrong with me. Nobody seemed to notice.

And sadly, I had to deal with it because this cousin was staying the night with us. And being that I am the only girl, she had to spend the night in my bed. That disappointed me because she had just violated me in a way that I was not expecting from a cousin. Because I never said anything to her like "I really didn't like that you kissed me," she continued these same behaviors every time she would spend the night. I hated this so much, but I was too afraid of speaking up for myself because she was a lot older than me. We even had to take baths together, and she would touch my vagina. I remember I would rush out of the tub so I could leave her in the bathroom. How is it that I'm taking a bath to get clean but I get out of the tub feeling dirty? Insane, I know.

Unfortunately, my story of molestation doesn't stop there. So, please tighten your seat belt as we travel down the timeline of unfortunate sexually abusive events.

I can remember on a Saturday night, a neighbor walks inside my room as I'm having my casual time alone; and he walks in and interrupts my alone time unannounced. He would say things like, "Kyshawna, what are you doing? I want to hang with you." As a child, I'm thinking to myself what does he need to play with me for? Nonetheless, as we begin to play with my brothers' toys, he says to me, "I am not going to hurt you; you are going to be fine." He told me to feel a certain way with his lips. But deep down in my core, I know this is not normal and that something is happening to me that should not be at all.

My heart is pierced, and I am frozen as he proceeds to touch me in places that were familiar from the last couple incidents that I had. All I can do is be left to my thoughts of fear, torment, confusion, wondering why this is happening and why would he do this to me. I never knew fear existed on a level like this and had no idea that this would become a repeated cycle for not just one, but many people in my life. The days of worrying about imaginary monsters came to an end because now I have to dread real ones, and they look just like me: HUMAN.

I should not have to feel like I was being physically punished just for wanting to be alone, especially as this same neighbor violated me repeatedly. I would dread every time the doorbell rang or there was a knock at the door. Over and over and over again, they just would not leave me alone; and I am too small to defend myself. I knew this was wrong and I needed to tell someone; but I knew that if I opened my mouth and told someone, nobody would believe me.

In the Black community, apparently if someone violates you sexually, it was your fault for letting it happen or being somewhere you should not have been. It makes absolutely no sense because I was not outside, but in my own home. I even found that I was no longer safe in my own bedroom because my neighbor would start sneaking into my room periodically and lay on top of me while I was asleep. These moments were very traumatizing. I can remember how fearful I felt when I felt the weight of this boy on top of me. I cannot fathom why all these people who do not even know me well felt like they could just take advantage of me.

By now, I have one image of what human monsters look like, but never in a million years could you have told me small people were capable of this kind of darkness as well. Not only was I violated and molested at home, but now my own classmates in kindergarten and first grade felt like they could touch me anywhere and everywhere as well. They must have known they were doing something inappropriate, for they would frequently request, "Please don't tell on me, Kyshawna." Little monsters must have unfortunately witnessed the same experiences from others in their households as well. So, like a germ, they do not know what to do with it instead of mimicking the learned behaviors.

By now, I am afraid to even hug my mother, grandmother, brothers and people who loved me with pure love. I was afraid that a simple hug or telling someone you loved them would turn into another moment of violation. I was already somewhat withdrawn from people; but now it is multiplied because I have to protect myself every moment of the day, even in my sleep. I am experiencing anger, confusion and all the psychological and emotional trauma that comes with being molested frequently. I feel out of place and scared out of my mind every day. I have nightmares when I am asleep, and I live out these same nightmares when I wake up.

At this point, I feel like I am hated by so many people to the point that I start hating things about myself. I began to feel less than a human being, less than pretty and that this was the only thing that I would know for the rest of these days. I used the bathroom in my bed more times than I can count because of the intensity of the nightmares I was having. It was so bad to the point that I would place my hand in my underwear when I went to bed just in case someone tried to touch me while I was asleep.

I was so afraid, that I allowed my brothers to take over my old room so that I could now sleep in the same bed with my grandmother so that I can feel a little safer. Maybe if I was with her, all the people who would dare try to touch me would finally be caught. By the time I was seven years old, my means of protection would now become a means of pleasure that I should have never known so soon or at all, in fact.

Late one night, I happened to be awake and walking around the house. There was no door in the room I used to sleep in. So, as I walked, I see my older brothers watching television. I am shocked, yet intrigued by what I see on the screen. Somehow, my brothers gained access to pornography and were watching people be with each other. They did not see me watching them. So, when they left, I walked into the room and continued watching it for myself.

These visuals began to awaken feelings and thoughts that I had never experienced. My hormones were awakened; and now I have another craving that, to me, is unnormal.

I started having dreams that emulated the various videos I watched. Since they had been etched into my memory and my heart and because I used to put my hand in my underwear to cover myself for protection, I now find myself placing my hands on my private part for pleasure. Between being exposed to molestation and pornography, masturbation was surely inevitable. This may not have happened as quickly if I did not have to protect my vagina every night. Maybe I felt it was safer to touch myself with permission than to let anyone else do so.

Anyone who has ever dealt with molestation, pornography or masturbation will know what it is like to walk in shame, fear, humiliation and isolation. Whether it is one or all three areas, you feel ashamed because people would potentially look at you differently and cringe every time they think about you. It, unfortunately, might cause others to attempt to take advantage of you because their twisted mindset is if you have been through it a lot, you must enjoy it. You dread how your family and friends would feel if they ever found out that you are involved in pleasuring yourself; and you, yourself, are too young to understand why you are even enjoying this.

It became an unhealthy coping mechanism to deal with the darkness and brokenness of my life and family. My family fights a lot. My mother cannot take care of me due to being sick from diabetes, and my own family members and classmates violate me frequently. My mom was there physically but not emotionally, so I could not talk to her. She would not be in the right headspace many times. So, even the simplest of conversations would turn into arguments. Not only can I not trust anyone with what happened to me, but now I also refuse to trust them with the secrets of what I have done to myself. Even in therapy, I could not talk. I felt silenced by my sorrow and shame. The only safety and security that I can find at this point in my life is by partaking in the same thing that causes me shame.

I felt singled out by the actions that I partook in. So, in my mind, I thought that if I were to speak out about my addictions and sexual abuse, I'd be judged and rejected. It is so unfortunate that at my young age, I knew what these things looked like, what shame looked and felt like. I lived with these secrets for so long, and it did nothing for me but hurt me continuously. I so deeply wanted help from my trauma but couldn't find the courage to speak out. I grew up being a mute child because of all the trauma I had experienced so quickly. Already being a shy person, being abused and needing someone to trust and tell my business seemed so impossible for me.

Experiencing molestation at 5-7 years old opened up my mind so fast to the things that were inappropriate. I hated this for myself because being so young, I should not have had to go through something so selfish and filthy. I never understood why someone did such a thing to me, always begging to hang out with me just so that they could touch on me. And I say "they" because it was never just one person who violated me. There were several neighbors and kids at school who did such.

I grew up knowing a lot of people in elementary school. I remember one day while in class, I asked my teacher if I could go use the restroom. And at this time, you needed a classmate to go with you. So, she sent me to the restroom with another girl. And this girl literally crawled underneath my bathroom stall and said to me, "Do you do this to your friends? Don't be scared because I do this to my friends." And she came up to me while I was still on the toilet and touched my breast and kissed my lips. Instantly, I went in shock mode; and she laughed at me and ran back to class. I went back in embarrassment because in my mind, I knew this was so messed up yet again. I can remember feeling so angry that someone had that much boldness to take advantage of me once again.

I was tired, frustrated and mad because it seemed as though this particular form of abuse just wouldn't give me a break. It was almost as if every time I turned around, there was a new face and a new gender seeking to abuse me. I couldn't come to terms why this was happening. And sadly, it just didn't stop there. All throughout my elementary years, I ran into someone molesting me either in the classroom or on the playground.

I can remember sitting at my desk in class; and the little boy that sat next to me would take his hand and rub it against my thigh. I would sit there and cry because something in me was so afraid to tell the teacher. I felt paralyzed and numb in the moment. I was stuck. I couldn't move. I couldn't speak. I was scared for my life. I felt like I was reliving the moments when my first molester took advantage of me. Being so afraid, I started feeling dumb, dumb because I wouldn't say anything, dumb because I felt it was my fault that these people kept touching me, dumb because nobody was catching these people violating me.

This shattered my heart and confidence into pieces. I knew none of this was my fault, but I couldn't accept the fact that I was scared. I didn't know what to do. All I knew was that I was tired, tired of the abuse at such a young age. Fighting perversions and physical abuse drove me insane. I would leave elementary and go to daycare and then go home, and every day it seemed like the same things were happening to me. And I was fighting these things alone because, again, I didn't feel safe enough to go tell anybody, not even someone my age.

I felt like the world was against me in these moments. I felt like no one understood me. All of this made me feel so singled out, alone, misunderstood and ashamed. And the crazy part about all this is that none of this was my fault. But that's how the enemy is; he makes it seem like what's done to us that is out of our control is our fault. And then he makes it seem like because you don't open your mouth and tell the people that you trust what's being done to you, that you must be okay with it. It's a sick, twisted situation. I had to be strong within to understand that bad things happen to those whom the enemy believes is powerful and is destined for greatness.

However, knowing these things didn't stop me from abusing me. Every time I kept my mouth shut about my abuse, I was hurting myself. Every time I would partake in pornography and masturbation, I was hurting myself. I mean being this young, I had no idea I was hurting myself. However, I did know what I was feeling. Gosh, my feelings were so hurt that I became numb to where I started to believe that this was just a part of life, my life, to be exact.

It caused me to be very sheltered within and even outwardly. I would dress as if it was winter every single day because wearing long sleeve shirts and pants covered up my skin. You see, molestation makes one think as though if just a little bit of skin is showing, that maybe someone who looks at it will have perverted thoughts about my skin. I know this was just a mental struggle of mine, but dressing completely covered up allowed me to be safe from people in some weird way.

Selfish Betrayal

U sually the narrative of homes with an absent parent is that the missing mother or father either did not want anything to do with the partner or the children. If the parent is alive and not present, more times than not, their names are slandered in the sight of the children. And it is truly heartbreaking when family forsakes family.

There is another side to this coin of abandonment that many refuse to discuss. What do you do about the parent or family member who has been exiled from communicating with their children while they actually have a yearning to be involved in their children's lives, even in the slightest way possible? I am a personal witness of having a parent who actually desired to be involved in my life but was denied access by the rest of my family, but mainly by my grandmother. What is even more disheartening about my scenario is that they tried to lie and hide about who this person was to me and make me think I was crazy for knowing the truth.

Contrary to popular belief, it is still possible for someone to at one point or another be raised in a two-parent home and it still be filled with chaos and dysfunction. I vividly remember one particular day around the time I was five or six years old, I overheard my mother yelling and arguing, which is something I wasn't used to, especially from my mother because she was a peaceful person. I caught her in a moment of disappointment. However, the statement that comes from her mouth next would shake me to my core. My mother exclaimed the words, "Kyshawna is not even your real daughter!" What is a child supposed to do with a statement like that? The man whose name is written on my birth certificate along with my mother is not even my biological father? All I could do from this point on is ask within myself, "Who is my real father? Where is my real father? Why is this man pretending to be my father, and why is my actual father not here instead?"

For the first few years of my life, this "substitute father" took care of my mother and was more financially stable than her. My mom, unfortunately, struggled to take care of us because of the lack of financial support. And then the fact that I was the fifth of her five children, it was hard on her. She had her medical condition that would further limit the resources she had access to in order to take care of us, not to mention her long history with drug addiction.

Her partner was already involved in her life by the time she was prepared to give birth to me, so he was willing to have his name written on my birth certificate, which is why I have my last name today.

I would receive money and gifts from him all the time for reasons I'll probably never understand. He wasn't emotionally available. It was almost as if I really didn't know who he was. He never showed me the emotional side that I knew was there. It was really interesting. In fact, I'd like to believe he gave me money and gifts all the time as an attempt to make up for the fact that he was unavailable emotionally. I'm sure he had his own struggles within that couldn't quite allow him to show his emotions. Growing up, I thought it was just a male thing.

I could never talk to him about his life and the trials he went through, and I never understood why he would never be open enough to talk to me and actually get to know me. I figured it was because he had his own issues, like his drug addictions. That's all I remember him really suffering from.

I remember riding in the car with him a lot. We'd go run errands, get food, buy clothes and go visit his side of the family. But I can see it so vividly right now, sitting in the car with him, he'd be high off some drug, which put me in danger because he was driving me around while intoxicated and even going as far as threatening to throw me out of the car. He would say things like, "Get out, get out the car."

And I would instantly start crying out of fear. I would look at him and almost not be able to recognize him because he wasn't like that when he was sober, which is how I could tell when he was high. I would sit there extremely scared of him. And then he would say, "I'm just playing, girl." I didn't fall for it because he did it too frequently. I would hate it when he would take me with him because he was always high and placing me in danger. And at my young age, I shouldn't be put in situations like that.

Moments like that made me think if that was how my biological father was because, as a child, my family, who didn't mind telling me the truth, would tell me my real father was a drug addict as well. It made me feel saddened on the inside because knowing that my parents were not sober people made me feel like I was robbed of the real experience of what parents are supposed to be like.

Nonetheless, to get back to the real point here, my substitute father's relationship with my mom brought unnecessary burdens and generational turmoil that is not even part of my genetic makeup. Money can always be replenished, but you will never regain the time that you lost. Gifts can never replace the grief you put someone through, and presents will never replace the presence I needed from a father figure in my life. He was there, but just as an obstruction rather than a blessing. I was grateful for the gifts and financial provision that kept us afloat. But the same way a circle can never fill a triangle-shaped void, he could never replace what I needed from my biological father.

Every time I would ask my mother, grandmother and other family members about my actual father, they would get upset and swear that I needed to look no further than the man whose last name I carried. But while my immediate family members were tight-lipped about my father, everyone on the outside was easily willing to share with me what I needed to know.

Warren Sterling Harris was often addressed by his

nickname Bunny; and everyone knew he was my real father, no matter how much my family tried to manipulate my mind into thinking otherwise. Unfortunately, there was a lot of drama and instability when he and my mother were together and conceived me, both of them using drugs frequently, which would add complications to my birth and health growing up. My grandmother wanted him away from us for good. He was forbidden to come see me, and I was forbidden to ask about him. But in my heart, I hoped that things would change.

I am grateful for the one aunt in my family who actually sympathized with my desire to see and meet him. When I was around the age of six, going on seven, my aunt would secretly take me to visit him; and we could not tell anyone because we would never hear the end of it from my grandmother if she found out. The first time we drove up to meet him, she took me by the hand as we walked up to this mobile home. Some of the longest 10 seconds of my life occurred once she knocked on the door.

And as we waited for him to open the door, not knowing what to expect, he opened the door; and our eyes locked for the first time. I can remember his eyes filled with a spectrum of emotions as he hugged me for the first time. I really wished with that first hug that I could have felt the same emotions he did. I did not feel scared, but I did not feel happy either. I didn't feel anything at all. I was in total shock.

I was greatly confused because of how I had been told that my father was the one dating my mother and why it would take so long for the real deal to see me. The sad truth is that not only was I hidden by my mother and grandmother's family, but he too was demanded to keep me a secret from his biological family as well. It was so sad that one day my dad's siblings told me that they had no idea their brother had another child because of how my grandmother didn't want him to be a part of my life. They too were convinced that their brother didn't have another child because of the lies and chaos that surrounded my mother's pregnancy concerning my father.

I was in awe because at this first moment, this is a stranger that just happens to share resemblance to me and happened to have been part of my creation. Other than that, there was not much to absorb from that moment. The one thing that made his hug special in spite of how numb I felt was that this was the first safe embrace I had from a male that I can remember. Being molested and violated by so many people up until now had caused me to feel uneasy when someone tried to show physical displays of affection. This is one of the first times someone gave authentic love to me instead of taking from me without permission. I guess this is how a father shows love, how a real man shows love.

There was not much for me and him to discuss due to me being so young, other than the questions that most parents and guardians ask their children, the simple questions of how I have been doing, how my day and week is going, what I have been up to and maybe what I want to be when I grow up.

He remarked at the little purse I always carried with me, and he promised he would make sure there was always something in there every time I saw him. He would give me all kinds of gifts, toys and money whenever my aunt took me to visit him. He would always tell me "A lady should never be broke, and a lady should always be taken care of." It would be some of the only peaceful moments I would have in this stage of life. Every time I went, I wished I could have stayed and never left again. He paid attention to me, listened to me and made me feel like I was the light and star of the room. I never had to fight for his energy or love. I just had to fight to see him.

I enjoyed the moments I got to see him, for he too would lavish me with money and gifts every chance he got. I could see and feel the same void in his heart that I had in mine. He was not another statistic of a parent that did not care about the child they left behind. He yearned to be in my life. He needed me just as much as I needed him. He might have made a lot of mistakes and bad decisions in his life, but I was his pride and joy; and my existence probably gave him a sense of purpose. I am sure he felt like a prisoner, only seeing me a few times as our hands touched the glass window of shame, the shame that plagued us.

I know it suffocated my father's heart that he was in a metaphorical house arrest and that we had to keep one of the most important connections of our lives a huge secret. Unfortunately, I can count on my hand the times that I saw my father before his life was cut short from an asthma attack. You would think my family would break the news to me, but I once again found out from people outside of home. I asked my mother about his asthma attack, and she said she knew the day it happened; but apparently, she did not feel it was important enough for me to know. If I cannot expect my own mother to be upfront with me, then who in the world could I trust at this point?

The man I always needed was literally stolen from me by sickness and secrets. Instead of memories, all I am left with at this point are questions and regrets. Questions of why didn't they think twice of the damage they were causing in my life at such a young age? Why didn't they see that he was a man who wanted to be a father to his youngest daughter? Why did they think my substitute father was way more equipped to care for me when they weren't really any different from one another?

I mean they were both drug addicts. The only difference is my biological father stopped his drug addiction, and my substitute father continued his struggle of drug abuse all my life. He was just a functioning addict.

Why did they allow one man's lack of financial status to get in the way of him being a present father in a little girl's life? I had so many questions; but I never once asked any of these questions for peace sake. And then too, I was very young.

So here I am dealing with the loss of my father and him being absent in my life for selfish reasons out of his control. I remember finding out the day he passed away, my little heart was shattered. It shattered because all I could think of is if I was given the privilege to hang with my dad for seven years of my life, maybe things would have gone differently. I had thoughts going through my mind day in and day out. I was broken because I just knew that things would have turned around for me if he was in my life. I thought maybe if he was present, I would have never experienced sexual abuse; that maybe if he was in my life, I wouldn't be suffering depression and anxiety as a child.

Suffering from the fear of abandonment emotionally and physically made me become isolated emotionally. I never desired to open up to anyone because of how depressed and how disappointed I was in the people who I thought were supposed to keep it real with me from the get-go. Betrayal was evident, and I couldn't accept the fact that this had to go down the way that it did. Had I known the real reasons as to why he was robbed from me at the time, I would have spoken up and stated how I felt. Never take a child's father away from them because of their struggles and the lack thereof.

Her Internalized Diagnosis

No one can physically touch your brain or heart unless they're a medical surgeon who cuts you open. Outside of the hospital, the slightest exposure or touch of your vital organs can cause permanent damage that could possibly end everything. Many people think that physical altercations and accidents are the only things that can injure or wound a person. They think those are the only circumstances that can trigger post-traumatic stress disorders; if only people would tread more lightly with not just their hands but also their mouths and non-physical actions.

The old saying goes, "Sticks and stones may break my bones, but words will never hurt me." Unfortunately, that is a complete lie. Words can cause major damage equivalent to the impact of a fist or a weapon. Each time someone calls you out of your name, it makes you feel less than human or disregards your basic needs for affection and affirmation. It can literally cause emotional turmoil and disease that stems from your troubled heart. You may know people who have little to no scars on their body, but you have no idea how many scars rest upon their psyche and soul.

By the ages of nine to eleven years old, the invisible barbwire that I had to continue walking through increased even more after my father passed away. I still had my mother in my life, but my grandmother was my primary caregiver; and I was a foster child under her watch. While the environment of a foster home is supposed to be stable and secure, there was a plethora of complications that gave me levels of stress that no child is physically or mentally able to handle.

I lost count of how many times I was hungry. It was not because there was no food, but many people in the neighborhood came in and out of the house swiping more food than they needed; and, to my knowledge, my grandmother allowed it. She was the neighborhood grandma who looked after everybody that came by the house. But what baffled me the most was that she did not extend that same behavior to me. Instead, I would have to countlessly ask her for food when I would get hungry and

I was denied access to food.

I remember feeling angry because how could someone who took me in to care for me and then not feed me when I asked for food. I mean clearly, I was hungry. This is when I discovered that I was receiving rejection: Rejection from being properly taken care of and properly loved. I would go to school, and I would ask my friends for some of their food. I remember looking at the concern in their faces. Their faces had the question of Why is she always hungry? Is she not eating at home?

It wasn't that I wasn't eating at home, but I ate when my grandmother felt the need to feed me. And, to my understanding, that's negligence. Could you imagine how embarrassed I felt at the lunch table asking my friends for some of their food? I dreaded hanging with my friends during lunch because I didn't want them to keep finding out that I wasn't eating like I should have at home.

A child should always be treated with proper care. They should be fed, clothed, loved and embraced. Unfortunately, I didn't receive all that growing up in my grandmother's household. For selfish reasons, I'll never get an understanding. She treated me a lot differently than she treated my siblings. It was almost as if she didn't want me as happy as they were. I saw it in her actions and heard it in her voice. She would speak to me with such negativity, like "That's why you're retarded and will never be anything." I ate more of her negative words than I did an actual meal, and it played on my mind to the point that I started to believe everything negative she said about me.

I used to believe that I was dumb because that's all I heard. I can't tell you one time my grandmother told me that I was smart, like how she did my brothers. I'd sit there fighting back tears because all I wanted was to receive that same praise and love she so faithfully showed my siblings. It played on my esteem to where I had none. I became so self-conscious of everything about myself that I believed that what she said about me was true.

I knew growing up that I was different, that I looked different because I was skinny and had a gap between my teeth. According to the kids, growing up, I wasn't considered the prettiest girl in school like most girls I saw around campus. Apparently because I was considered an outcast to most, I was picked on and bullied a lot. I remember being called buckteeth, Bugs Bunny, skinny girl and weirdo. Nobody really seemed to embrace the fact that I was human just as they were, and it was because I didn't meet the attractiveness that they saw around them.

Both girls and boys picked on me because they felt they could. They'd push me around. If I wouldn't react to their harsh words, they would throw things at me at recess and take toys and jump ropes from me. They didn't want me to be happy; instead, they wanted me to be miserable just like them.

School weighed down on me with all of the bullying and negative stigmas placed upon me by my grandmother, the students and my teachers. My grades were poor, as I could never seem to get above a C in my classes and on tests. It was not because I wasn't intelligent; but rather, I was unfocused because all I could think about was the negative words these people spoke over me. It is hard to focus on words and numbers on paper when your mind is clouded with thoughts like whether or not I'm smart. My performance in school caused the teachers and staff to place me on an individualized education plan, which caused my peers to think I'm "special," dumb, retarded and so many other ignorant statements.

Many people were certain that I would become part of a statistic that claims I would never do well or accomplish anything worthwhile with my life, as my grandmother did. I was born with drugs in my system due to whatever my mother had used while carrying me. So, that further added more emotional and mental complications on me, which is something my grandmother knew. So, I never understood why she played on my struggles.

I had a speech impediment growing up, only furthering their low expectations of me. When you hear these toxic expectations and outcomes, after so long, you finally begin to believe that this is who you are and who you will always be.

My grandmother, more times than not, treated all of my family members better than me. I heard the same words in school and out of school. And nowhere was safe from the verbal abuse I endured every day. I can't even count on my fingers how many times she and others would call me slow, dumb and worthless. Instead of understanding my pain, grief and the handicaps I was born with and developed, their descriptions of me would just become more fuel for the ice-cold needles that were spewn from their words.

To be told that no one had hope for me or believed in

me only caused me to hate myself and my life, not seeing a future or an existence outside of what I was handed. I could not even jot down my thoughts on paper due to the inability to write at that point. So, it is like being trapped in the prison of your generational dysfunction.

Had I known their words and actions towards me was just a reflection of how they felt about themselves, I would have ignored them. But because I didn't know this, I wore their words on my sleeve. It had become a part of my identity. As their words entered my ears and into my heart, they influenced my actions in ways I would not have imagined. I started to hate school to the point I would not do my homework and wouldn't study. I eventually started ditching classes. I felt like I wasn't capable of staying the course and being smarter than my decisions. But oh, well. Right? It wasn't like anyone cared enough about me for me to do what was right anyways. That was my approach to the situation.

Children should have several outlets in their lives where their dreams, aspirations and imaginations are allowed to flourish. You should be able to explore what you like, what you dislike and the thoughts that make you desire a reality that is bigger than the daily challenges that stand before you. One of the most painful things you can experience is having your dreams crushed before you can even formulate them. There is a new level of mind control where the only dream you have is the dream of despair and destitution birthed by the opinions, statistics and expectations of everyone around you.

Everything around me by now is exploding on the outside while I implode on the inside. I may still have a mother, grandmother and brothers; but by this point, I still feel isolated. It is very possible to be surrounded and still be alone. I would spend several years carrying the darkness of every word and moment of neglect on my entire person, mind, body and soul. Right now, for this little girl, dreams, hopes and joy are only luxuries that could never be obtained.

You'd think with already having a tough upbringing that people would desire to pour love and positivity in me as much as they could. The actions and judgments of these kids, teachers and my family put so much fear and sadness in my heart that I hated myself so much because nobody in my life seemed to want to accept me for who I was or for how I looked.

I grew up a tomboy and was labeled gay for it, gay because I dressed covered up and comfortable, gay because nobody wanted to date me. It bothered me to the point I'd hide during breaks and in classrooms. I'd sit next to my teachers because I felt they'd protect me, but I was wrong. Some teachers allowed the students to bully me right before their eyes. I couldn't believe it. One day, a student threw a pencil at my head and called me skinny-dip; and the whole class laughed, right along with the teacher. All I could do was lay my head down, and I never lifted my head up again until class was over.

From that day onward, I always walked with my head down. Life to me was pointless. I felt the pressure of life rush through my body, and I wanted so badly to die. I didn't see the need to live anymore because, honestly, how much can a kid take? Being bullied at home, daycare and school was a lot for my heart to take. I allowed what everybody thought of me to crowd my mind and take me to this very dark place called "suicidal thoughts." I know that's pretty dark, huh?

I mean let's be truthful here. Many people deal with

suicidal thoughts when they lose hope and a sense of purpose. Clearly I did, but I am thankful that I didn't let myself go to where I started to act on the negative thoughts that were crowding my mind.

One day I woke up and felt a weight lifted off my shoulders. I had no clue on how it happened. All I can remember was how peaceful I started to feel. I got up that day and decided that I would no longer allow these people to belittle and bully me. I had told myself there must be something special about me and my existence if everyone seems to have a problem with it, and I was right. I began to gain a confidence I never knew I could gain nor feel.

I started to wear my confidence, and people at school started to see it. I started to be nice to the people that were mean to me, which confused them. I would offer them my snacks that I'd been given by the school staff. And because of this sudden shift, people started to look at me differently. They slowly but surely started to like me. But I'd like to believe that these same people always did like me; but because people would be mean to the "unique" girl, it influenced them to treat me as they saw others treat me.

I stopped allowing things to bother me by finding ways

to encourage and love myself for who I was. I believed in my heart that God created me in His image and in His likeness. And if people didn't agree nor see that, then that just wasn't my problem.

Transformed Identity

F amily is a beautiful thing when structured correctly, and it is not always about being related by blood or having the same parent or grandparent. A true authentic family can come in many forms, such as friends from school, people with similar hobbies and interests and people who love you and look out for you in ways you don't even know that you need. It is not always easy looking for groups of people whom you can truly feel connected to and be not only loved, but also be able to trust them.

However, when you finally find safe places and homes away from home where you can be free and be yourself, it truly is paradise in the midst of all of your problems. There is much healing and security when you come across someone or some people who do not care about your past, your flaws and the parts of your biological background that bring shame and the fear of being judged or criticized. When you meet people who help push you into love and destiny, you gain a new sense of purpose, a new level of joy and you feel like you have a brand-new name.

By this point in time, I am eleven years old and existing, not even living anymore. I have become so accustomed to the abuse at home, the rejection of family members and being labeled as a failure in school for which my teachers had no hope for. Nothing is my norm, and I have learned to accept that this may be all that I am and all that I will ever know. I feel trapped in trauma and muzzled in misery and that there will never be a way out of this prison. I would do anything just to feel the slightest amount of joy, but it is so dark even on days full of sunshine.

I had family and I had associates from school and around the area, but never a true friend who I could rely on and lean on without being afraid or distrusting. All of this would finally change during the year of 2007. This would be the year that I make my first true friend and find a new path for myself where I would begin to go through a metamorphosis and blossom into the real me that has been buried underneath the mud of my past.

A new family moved on the block I lived on during 2007, and I had no idea how their presence would change my life. It was through these neighbors that I would finally make my first real friend. She was a year or two older than me, and she became the sister and one of the positive female influences that I needed in my life.

You see, up until now, the word "friends" was just a filler word for the people in my life who I hung around; but I knew deep in my heart that they were not what I truly needed and longed for. They honestly were one-sided friendships, as I pretended that they could fill the voids, knowing that they smiled in my face but never really cared. They wanted to drag me into negative circumstances to humiliate me even more. What was worse is that they were close with the same people who bullied me throughout my years in school. So, there was no way I could trust them with the secrets of my heart, for they would probably tell those who wanted to hurt me so they can use it as fuel for their ridiculing and spewing of evil words about me and my issues.

So, it felt amazing to finally experience what a true friend was like, the blessing of having a human angel who loved you and cared about you and saw you past the most humiliating areas of your life, which was priceless. It would be through people like her that I would learn to slowly but surely trust in people and be able to believe that I am loved, I am valued and that I am worthy of having friends and people who love me just because, without ulterior motives and wicked plots.

It was on one Friday evening that I noticed this van outside of my friend's house picking her up. Out of curiosity, I ran outside to the vehicle to see who was picking her up and where they were going. The van was filled with children and teenagers, bubbling with excitement and joy; and they seemed to really enjoy each other's company. I asked the driver of the van where they were taking my friend and all of these other kids, and the driver said they were on their way to church.

I had no idea what I was getting myself into, but all I knew was I really wanted to go and see what all of the excitement was about. Because if all of these kids are going, it must be fun and it must be safe. I asked if I could come along, and they were delighted to take me. I had no idea that when I placed my foot inside the bus and took a seat that I would embark on a beautiful journey of healing, purpose and confidence.

My first night ever in church was nothing major, but it was a simple moment that would increase a hunger and a longing that I never knew I could fulfill. They did not have a service the night I attended, but it was a choir rehearsal; and it opened up my mind and heart to so many possibilities for me and gave me a glimpse of my potential. The songs that the youth choir practiced were beautiful and harmonious, and I wanted to be included in releasing those melodies from my lungs. I loved singing all kinds of music, for singing would be one of the few escapes and moments of serenity I would have from everything I was going through. I had some natural talents such as singing, dancing and even acting that would keep me strong.

So now, I had a safe place to let my creativity flow from my being. I started singing with the choir, beginning to understand why these songs filled them with such joy and excitement. The more I would sing and practice these songs, the more I would feel such love and peace that I had waited my whole life for. These kids were not just singing to the wind, but every song was meant for two types of people. The melodies were meant for those who came to church who would be going through diverse problems and burdens that you can sometimes see written on their faces. It would help them cry out and let go of the inner turmoil and the anxiety that their lives were causing them, being able to return to their homes, schools and places of employment with enough strength to endure until they came back for another service the following week.

The second type of person were those who received these anthems of hope and love into their hearts. If you have ever been to church or are familiar with church culture, you have probably heard the name Jesus. He is also referred to by the names God, the Lord, Jehovah and Yahweh. Many might not understand it; but His presence is so real, beautiful and powerful, even though you can't see Him, outside of the various depictions of Him in church drawings, windows and Biblical documentaries on television. But if you ever get a chance to feel His love and know Him, it will change your life forever.

I did not consider myself a Christian just yet even though I had been coming to many choir rehearsals and services by now. All I knew was that this church was a safe place and that the feelings I would get in my heart while coming to these services and singing these songs were like none I had ever felt before. I wouldn't trade it for anything. It was not until a series of youth services that the church had in the summer that I would make a decision to become a Christian. The first night of the service was amazing, especially as I listened to the preacher that evening. Up until now, I really struggled with remaining focused and paying attention for long periods of time, mainly because of all of the turmoil and voices running through my mind.

However, I became completely captivated by everything the preacher spoke that fateful evening. I cannot remember word for word what he said, just that I was able to fully grasp the context of everything shared due to being mature so early on in life. The basis of the majority of the church's messages are what we call the Gospel or "Good News," which declares that Jesus loves us as we are and that nothing we have ever done or said would keep Him away from us if we ever wanted to know Him and befriend Him.

God came to earth as a man so that He could fully identify with the many concerns and crises that we endure in our earthly existence; and He went so far as to pay the price of death, which would cause every mistake and everything we would ever do wrong to be forgiven. This message of unconditional love caused me to feel like a pair of hands wrapped themselves around my heart and began to heal and mend everything going on inside of me.

When the preacher closed his Bible and finished his sermon, he asked if there was anyone who would like to know Jesus as a Savior and as a friend. As my heart was filled with a love I never knew, and as the tears flooded my eyes and poured down my cheeks, I ran to the front of the church crying out repeatedly with every fiber of my being, "Jesus, save me! Jesus, save me! Jesus, save me!" With every tear that left my eyes, one by one, I began to feel the weight of my wrongdoings and the iniquities inflicted upon me leave my shoulders and my body. I was saved from my fears, saved from the shame that I carried and saved from every curse and negative word spoken over me at home, school and in my community.

As I wept and unloaded every unshed tear from the last 7-12 years of my life, the preacher began to talk about my future. The Lord is referred to in Hebrews 12:2 as "...the author and finisher of our faith." So, He knows everything about us, even the places we wish He did not notice. His love and power are so great that He can take everything that has happened to you and reverse their emotional, physical, psychological and spiritual effects on you.

The Lord shared with the preacher about how much He loves me and how precious I am to Him. The preacher also said that I would be doing the same thing he does, for the Lord desired to use me to spread His love through preaching His word. As this was all going on, I heard His voice for the first time ever; and the Lord said unto me, "From this day forward, your life will never, ever be the same."

After the preacher was done ministering to me, some of the church leaders took me to another room where I could continue to just weep and wail and let everything out that I had been holding onto for my entire life. The love of the Lord flooded my soul, washing away and flushing out my shame, my sin and my low self-esteem. Everything and anything that I had done wrong before that night, I no longer had a desire to do them.

Many people who were placeholders for true and authentic friendships and meant me no good whatsoever, I was ready and able to let them go. My musical appetite would begin to change as well, consisting of many of the songs I heard during the church services.

There were a few more nights of this youth gathering. So, every night, I kept running to the front of the church for prayer. It seemed like every time I walked up there that weekend, I wept and wept as the Lord removed so many burdens, habits, addictions and mindsets that kept me in bondage.

I spent so many years feeling lost and confused, not knowing who or what I was. Now, I can identify myself not as a failure, a victim or a child with special needs; but now, I can proudly declare that I am a daughter of God. The God who created everything loves me and makes time just to know me and speaks to me. His friendship filled many voids that I had been looking for people to fill and to love me and embrace me. Being that I was overlooked and rejected everywhere else, He was my new family. And the church that I ended up at was my new family. Where I lived was a house, but not a home. Through Jesus and the church, I finally had a home.

My favorite place in the world was my church, and I spent so much time there for the remainder of 2007 into 2010. I sang with the youth choir on every third Sunday of the month, and I started participating in the dance ministry as well. These outlets were therapeutic and crucial aspects of my growth and healing, and I spent more time here than I did at home. I was probably the first one there and the last one to leave. I was at every single service throughout each week, including midweek Bible studies and choir and dance rehearsals. And whenever our pastor or leaders fellowshipped and ministered at various churches in our community, I was there.

We even had an outreach group, and our goal was to go to the streets as a team and share God's love with the homeless, people in the stores and even on blocks where drug and gang activity were prevalent. I was so on fire and passionate for the Gospel that I was not even afraid to go into those areas. I was so determined to give people a chance to feel the same love I did, there was no room for fear any more. There was even one time where we had a contest of being able to bring the most people to the church and to the Lord, and I won when I brought over 30 people from the streets, school and my family. The work of ministry and being a preacher started to manifest itself in moments like those.

I spent so much time with the Lord in church that year that I began to undergo some serious transformations in my mind and heart. It started with no longer dressing like my older brothers and becoming more feminine in my wardrobe, spreading love and not walking in excessive anger like I used to do. I also obtained the discipline to no longer pleasure myself with pornography and masturbation. I had no idea I could be changed into a new girl and that I was royalty and being adorned from the inside out.

By the end of 2007, I experienced a radical transformation that we call in church culture as "being filled with the Holy Spirit." The Holy Spirit is another name for the Lord. And what happens is He becomes one with us, and we are able to walk in a deeper fellowship with Him that is not limited to just coming to church. The Lord is probably the greatest friend you can ever have. So, being tied to the Holy Spirit gives you so much clarity and wisdom about who God is, who you are, who the people in your life are and where to place them.

There are many powerful benefits to being full of God that will change many lives when you get to that point of knowing Him. One of them is being able to speak in a

Heavenly language, which is what happened to me when I started walking closely with Him. Talking in a Heavenly language or "speaking in tongues" is not gibberish or babble, but it is a supernatural combination of every language ever uttered throughout the world and throughout history because the Lord is omnipresent.

He allows us to deal with issues and matters that do not just affect us but the entire world at large. As we communicate with God through this aspect, we gain miraculous wisdom, knowledge and even glimpses into the future of ourselves and the futures of others, according to the plan of God. This helps us pray so that we know how to sometimes address things that can only be seen and noticed through the eyes of the Lord.

Walking in the Lord is so powerful because when I allowed Him to light the candle of my heart with His presence, I started walking in gifts I never knew I had. The words of the preacher came to pass in the coming months. As I started speaking and preaching during church services, my grades began to improve, for now the supernatural intelligence of the Lord allowed me to grasp and understand a lot of the things in class that were once impossible for me due to the many mental hindrances I was born with.

As stated earlier, my desires and appetites changed drastically; and I knew I could live a life and present myself in a pure and powerful way that contradicted every expectation of those around me. I knew I was not perfect, but that I could be righteous because that is the nature of my Father God in Heaven.

My relationship with God began to rub my family members the wrong way because I spent more time with Him and His people than them. I lost a chance to truly have my natural father, but I was not going to allow anything to keep me from my Heavenly Father.

Even though my natural name never changed, there was something different now when my name was called. When the Lord or people in my church said my name, there was a rush of joy, purpose and beauty. I have an invisible crown, and I am now understanding my royalty.

When God came into my life, it felt as if He instantly changed my life from top to bottom; and it was done at the most perfect time. As you already read, I was dealing with such heartache that it was causing me to self-sabotage myself to the point that I couldn't even look myself in the mirror because I hated myself. I hated how I looked, how I talked, how skinny I was. I hated my entire existence because of how badly I allowed what people and the enemy thought and said to me. Nobody could convince me that I was beautiful, important, worthwhile, amazing and strong because I accepted what negative people said instead of what God said.

Giving my life to God on July 17, 2007 was one of the best decisions that I ever made in my 11 years of life. God knew that He needed to change my heart, transform my mind, my appearance and restore my confidence. Though it was a process, He touched my heart and mind the minute I submitted to who He wanted to be in my life; and that was to be my Heavenly Father.

The Influenced 7 Transition

I wonder what it would be like if caterpillars could talk and communicate with each other. Those first seasons of life are slow and difficult, being dragged down by not only gravity but everything that you hold on the inside of you. It is one thing to be weighed down by the pressures of your pain and purpose combined; but there is such liberty when you get to the place like a caterpillar, when you are able to rise above the pressure and soar freely without worrying about crawling in chaos for the rest of your life.

The caterpillar goes through a season of metamorphosis, as it loses a lot of its weight and legs; and then it takes the true form of the butterfly that was encoded in its biology. I always wondered if caterpillars looked at butterflies with envy, wishing that there was some way they could clip their wings, for the butterflies still see them as the same old caterpillar who was just crawling with them a few moments ago.

Insecurity will do that to you and make you attempt to fear what you do not understand and will force someone to change back into how you knew them before their transformation. What is so amazing is that caterpillars can never produce offspring in their initial stages. It is only until they become a butterfly that they are able to produce after their own kind. That is why you must push to maintain your change and never allow anyone to take it from you because your transformation can and will produce hope and purpose in the caterpillars of your life.

I am loving the young woman I have become, the me I was always meant to be in the plan of God. My transformation was so sudden and so rapid that to many people, it looked like I evolved overnight. Being in church and walking with the Lord was so good for me, and it gave me fresh new air to breathe into my lungs. I had a reason to live again, to laugh again, to love again; and this joy and confidence flowed from my being and touched every area of my life.

I used to have many arguments with family members and lash out in anger, but I began to have a bit more compassion when dealing with their disagreements and sharp tongues. I continued to grow in ministry as I sang, danced and preached, both inside and outside the church, because I wanted everyone to know God the same way I did and have a new sense of purpose that goes beyond whatever they may be currently facing.

It honestly confused and bothered my grandmother on how I changed so drastically in less than a year. She probably thought I was brainwashed or going through an emotional phase that would not last long, but all she knew was that I spent more time in church than at home. You would think that being in a safe place like church and not on the street corner or hanging out with gangs or bad influencers would make her proud and secure, knowing that I am growing well and not getting into trouble. At the moment, she still saw the caterpillar I used to be, crawling and weighed down by everything that has happened in my life.

Since family sees you almost every day, they become so familiar with you and can rarely honor or appreciate when you begin to go in a direction they never expected or that goes against what they have done for decades and generations. I started to gain wings, and maybe the flapping of my wings was making too much noise for my family. But I know as I continued to flap my wings, they would fan in much needed fresh air into our lives.

By the summer of 2008, I had been attending church for a full year now and was looking forward to a summer spent at my favorite place. One Sunday, as I got dressed and headed outside so that my neighbor who works at the church could pick me up for service, my grandmother decided to tell my neighbor that she will no longer permit me to go to church anymore. She conjured up a handful of lame excuses on why I was not allowed to attend, including that she does not know what is going on there, that I have endless chores around the house and that I am still struggling with my schoolwork and needed ample time to work on my math.

As the door closed and my neighbor had to proceed to church without me, my heart was shattered. All I could do was scream and cry with frustration. It was a while since I really acted out or had a temper tantrum, but I was ready to throw and break everything in sight because I had been caged and separated from my refuge.

Days and weeks would go by as I prayed and prayed for

my grandma to let me go back, but her decision was settled in her heart. I can recall pleading and begging her because she knows how hard my life has been and how I finally had a space to be free and to let out all of my grief. Basically, I was told that it is what it is and that I needed to get over myself and that I probably would return back to the way I was before I started going.

Faith does not make life easy, but it is like pushing your muscles to new levels of strength while exercising. It hurts when you lift up the heavy weights of believing that hope and love can change your life and your surroundings. But the more you push yourself, the stronger your muscles become. Like a butterfly, for someone to cut you open out of your chrysalis instead of letting you break yourself out, which will weaken you and make your wings soft, sometimes you have to push through and endure when things are not going your way.

Whether it was someone like me who wanted to desperately go back to church or for a dream school or a dream job you were turned down for, do not give up. I know personally that prayer and faith in a seemingly impossible outcome will go farther than asking a fellow human being will. Your faith can change minds and soften hearts so that no one and nothing stands between you and the desires of your heart.

One of the main reasons that I was able to survive my season away from the church was that my aunt would come by my grandmother's house often and would tell me to go inside my room and pray. I remember I would do as she instructed and could remember always crying every time I talked to God, and doing this every time I saw my aunt caused me to gain a burning desire to pray all the time. I knew my prayers touched Heaven because every time I prayed for a particular situation, I'd see God's hand move on the prayer. My aunt provoked my prayer life, and it is because of her that I knew when it was necessary to pray concerning a matter. So, while my grandmother would stop me from going to church, I turned to prayer because that's all I had to hold onto aside from my faith and hope in God.

Maybe it was actually good that I was forbidden from church for a season because even though I was hurt greatly by not being able to fellowship with the other congregants, I learned that the church experience and the fruit it should bear can still be cultivated at home during your day-to-day life.

While separated from my church, I did not feel separated from God. As a matter of fact, I began to hear Him more and more clearly as He would lead me to pray for certain individuals, situations and environments. He was training me to become attuned to His impressions and promptings that I would feel in my mind and heart and then act upon them accordingly. This way, when I would return to church one day, I would know when God is speaking and when someone is just talking out the side of their neck. There are many times where people will try so hard to act like God over your life. So, it was imperative for me to know what control and manipulation sounds like and looks like.

I knew my grandmother started to see me in a new light because her actions towards me started to change. Not fully, but little by little, she gained a tolerance for my presence. Though it still bothered her, I knew she knew that God was doing a quick and new work in me because when she would try and provoke me to react to her negative actions, I'd turn a cheek to the madness. And because I did not fall to the negativity that was presented, she knew that I had changed for the better and wanted to find out how this truly happened for me.

Before church, I was full of anger and silence and did not want to do much with anyone; but my heart slowly softened, and it remained that way while I was separated from church. My grandmother began to observe that I continually grew gentle and more compassionate and tolerant, causing her to rescind her decision of not allowing me to go. She would remark that she sees the church did change me after all and that it was not just an emotional experience or a phase. These changes in my attitude and personality were permanent, and I was not going to allow anyone or anything to turn me back into the ball of brokenness and bitterness that I used to be.

I stood my ground both vocally and silently, believing that one day my grandmother would finally understand my heart and my passion. Eventually, my public protests towards her and my silent prayers to the Lord would prevail as she finally, out of nowhere, had a change of heart and allowed me to start going to church again. Not only that, but my family all acquired an interest in the environment that caused such a radical change in my heart in such a short period of time. The woman who was once adamant about never letting me go to church again would now give her life over to the Lord. This turnaround would begin one by one, starting with my mother coming with me to church now.

Growing up, we went to church here and there but never on a consistent basis. Well, my mother did, but not the rest of my household. However, when my mother stopped going to church, I remember seeing her always praying in the morning and at night and reading her Bible from home. She was always so strong in the midst of all of her sicknesses, so I am pretty sure that is where she drew her strength from.

She started going to church with me, and her prayer and worship would continue to go higher and deeper with each service. She would cry out and give God glory for everything in spite of how hard life had torn her down, and it made me really proud to be her daughter. It solidified my own identity as a believer because, clearly, I come from the womb of a worshipper.

As I continued to invite my brothers, cousins, aunts and uncles, they would not only just visit once, but many of them ended up becoming members. I literally won my family over to God, and that gave me so much hope and healing. When my family started coming to my church, they were so eager to get ahold of what was so different about me. It was almost as if they wanted a taste of the same change that happened in my life. I remember seeing my family run to the altar for prayer and seeing them cry out to God just as I did when I first went to the altar.

First, it was my brother's reaction to God that shook me to the core. I had never witnessed my brother become vulnerable before a crowd of people. I had never witnessed him plead and cry out for forgiveness and change like I did on that Sunday morning. It made me so happy to witness the rebirthing of my brother's identity. But it doesn't stop there. My grandmother crying and asking for a complete change blew me away because all of my life, I had only known her to be very stubborn and bitter, which I know only comes from the hidden stories of her upbringing and childhood traumas. I thought I'd never see the day that this lady would break before God like I witnessed. It showed me that deep down in her heart, she really wanted to be changed from within. It just took a touch from God to break her down in an instance.

I had witnessed the prayers I uttered to God this day. I

had prayed countless nights that God would give my family the same burning desire, freedom and deliverance that He had given me. I could not dare be selfish and continue my life change and not take my family with me. I had come to the realization that God needed me to go back and get my family out of darkness and bondage so that they could be free as well. He used me to be the light and direction they so desperately needed, which I am grateful they were able to gain a new spiritual life as I did.

We were the largest family at our church and made our mark in the community, especially with many of us serving in various ministries, including my grandmother, who would cook food for the homeless. The beauty of my family experiencing God the way that they did caused them to remain hungry for that same experience Sunday after Sunday. It encouraged them to join the same church that I was committed to. I had prayed that they would find this place as home because that was what it was to me. I had longed for them to be where I was every Sunday because by doing that, we would have the chance to get closer to one another.

Growing up in a dysfunctional family, all one desires is

for their family to be mended together and to become closer. That was my heart's desire since a young girl. All I wanted was to have a family who wasn't afraid to be close, who wanted to love one another, who desired to have family time and to just be a beautiful family. God did just that for me. We were mended together again. I'd like to believe that it happened because of prayer and because we all now had something so powerful and common, and that was being newborn believers of Christ. We all would go to church together now, talk about it as we left and enjoyed family time back at home. It was amazing to see how God began to change the way my family was. Everybody seemed happier. They all found that there was something to look forward to, and that was Jesus.

My grandmother, mother and family watched me as I grew spiritually through singing, preaching and praying both regularly and through the Holy Spirit with other languages; and my fire was contagious and spread onto them. My metamorphosis into a Christian who fully embraced her newfound identity as a daughter of God caused my family to break free from the caterpillar mindsets of their sins, failures and generational bondages.

I am tangible evidence that it is never too late to give yourself and your family a new freedom and a new foundation. You can and will rebuild from the ashes of your agony, and your freedom can unmuzzle and unlock others from any and every lie and curse that has kept them bound.

The Sudden Loss

G rief is like a mosquito bite that catches you by surprise but lingers for a long time after your nerves catch up to what has taken place on your skin. You rarely feel or catch when the mosquito has latched onto you and pokes your arm with its needle of a mouth; but then a few hours or days later, a red blemish appears that is both painful to look at and is painful for your skin. It would be one thing if it either itches or hurts; but it is truly frustrating that it itches and hurts at the same, making comfort and relief almost impossible. You can use various ointments and creams to ease the pain; but nothing can make it go down. You have to endure it until one day it dissolves and your skin is back to normal.

How we deal with grief in certain stages of our lives depends on where we are mentally and spiritually, the nature of the passing and how close we are to the person or opposite. I say the opposite because sometimes you long for a stronger or deeper relationship with various individuals; and then it never comes, or you did not have enough time, leaving you with the agonizing question of what could have been if you had more time with them. The road of grief is so rocky and cannot be detoured or avoided, but learning how to ride the waves like the high ocean tides in the evening is key to staying afloat without drowning in despair.

It was one weekend in March that my life would change forever. I had a beautiful weekend coming up in church where I could just sit before God and worship and receive His love through the songs and messages three days in a row. I wanted to get my hair ready for the long weekend, so I asked my mother to help me do my hair. By this time, my mother has given her life to the Lord, along with other family members who were taking more of an approach to the culture of Christianity.

She has watched me for the last year blossom into a bold and beautiful woman inside and outside as I serve and sing in church, letting go of the many mindsets and patterns I grew accustomed to up until now. Our relationship started to heal, slowly but surely becoming what I needed her to be for me my whole life. Even something as simple as doing my hair was the bonding and quality time I longed for, especially having that woman figure who could speak life and love into me.

This time was different, for my mom expressed that she was feeling really tired. I told her she did not have to overexert herself to get my hair finished if she did not have the energy, but she insisted on doing my hair anyway. You know how mothers can be. They will continue attending to you regardless of how tired they are, and it is because they love you that much.

Afterward my mother did my hair, I went to church and had an amazing weekend of worship Friday, Saturday and Sunday. I had several weekends full of church activities that would keep me occupied and flourishing in my newfound purpose and identity. Sunday capped it off with some very powerful worship and preaching.

Life is so good right now. My grades are better, my family is slowly having a better change of heart towards me, I am healing with my mother and I have a wonderful relationship with the Lord. I was literally in the clouds as my life was changing beautifully. Many areas that were desolate and barren were now springing with life; and nothing could take this new joy that I have, that I always wanted and always needed.

I came home from church on Sunday evening to find my grandmother's house surrounded by cars, making me even more excited than I already was this weekend. I walked in the door expecting my family to have gathered for a last-minute party just to enjoy each other's company, not knowing what was awaiting me at the door. I greeted everyone and exclaimed to them one by one how beautiful my day was at church each day, but I started to notice they are unmoved and unusually quiet as I go on and on.

I ran to my brothers as well to greet them and to share my day with them, but that is when they looked puzzled at my excitement. "Nobody told you what happened yet? Mom is gone, sis," said one of my brothers. "What do you mean gone?" I asked. He said, "She passed away earlier today while you were at church." I honestly did not believe them and thought they were messing with my head. They said go back and ask everyone else in the kitchen. And, to my dismay, everyone confirmed that my mom was truly gone.

I was about to eat dinner, but then I ended up throwing my plate on the floor and hollering in disbelief. I was completely caught off guard and instantly became angered. First, I ran to my room and cried and cried on my pillow, for my heart had been snatched out of my chest yet again. I would then continue to weep and wail as I ran out the house and sat outside. All I could do is ask God why would he allow both of my parents to pass away so soon in my life. I barely had any time with either of them, and now I feel alone all over again.

As I poured my heart out in prayer, I heard the Lord say to my heart, "You are not alone, daughter. I will carry you through this moment. This is where I need you to trust me the most and trust me with everything you are and everything you have, which is faith." To think I would still be able to hear Him over the volume of my agony is astonishing, and I had no clue that He would be so near during this time.

His power kept me, while this new grief and the old wounds of losing my father began to open up. I could only sit there and feel the depths of my brokenness grow even deeper. Though I knew God was there, I was really angry because my mother was my everything. She understood me when nobody else did, and she talked me through every problem I had. I had just gotten closer to my mom; and to have her taken from me in the blink of an eye, I thought it was selfish of God to allow such a thing to happen to me. I thought I'd be able to grow up with my mom by my side, as we had had conversations weeks before her passing about the plans we had for one another and how we wanted to grow our relationship and spend more time together. I mean we would talk on the phone for hours about anything you can think of.

Before her passing, I wanted to tell her everything about my abuse, my secret struggles, my traumas, my flaw-led perspective of life and everything in the book; but I wasn't granted that chance. And because of that, I was mad. I was mad because I knew that if she would have gained the knowledge of all that I had gone through, I just knew she'd find ways to further protect me from the dangers of life, the perversions I was bound by, the molestation I had to fight off alone. I knew that if she knew, she'd be there to put a stop to it all. I remember feeling so lost without her in those moments. I had just gained the courage to trust her completely, and that was all I needed was to tell her everything that I was so afraid to shed light on.

I wanted to tell my mom things about my life that she was unaware of because I knew that she would understand where I was coming from. I learned that my story wasn't that far off from hers. My mother grew up amongst seven other siblings, her mother and father. She too dealt with the monsters of sexual predators. She mentioned to me that she was molested a lot growing up, as well as even being raped. According to the conversations I had with my mother, she expressed to me that her childhood was pretty rough, growing up in poverty, suffering from several forms of abuse, being bullied and also being an outcast.

My mother shared with me how she dealt with the loss of her father, as well as I did. She told me one night when we talked about my dad passing away, she mentioned how she could relate to the pain she saw in my eyes. She knew how hard it would be for me growing up not really knowing and experiencing the fullness of who my dad was because of him not being in my life. The only difference with my dad and my mom's dad was that my mom's dad was a part of her life. She mentioned to me that he was there up until he passed away. He died of a chronic illness just as my dad did. We had that part in common, which made my process go a lot smoother because I had someone there to nurture me in times of uncertainty and grief. She was literally my rock.

Her death really made me mad because I never would have imagined that just six years later, I'd lose my mom so unexpectedly and suddenly just as I did my dad. Life at that moment did not have much meaning to it. I didn't see an end or a positive outcome to the death of my parents. I questioned it a lot, even when I knew that better days could possibly be ahead if I responded to the situation the correct way; and I was correct. I leaned on the foundation that was laid out for me, and that was my relationship with God.

He kept me afloat and focused on being strong in my moment of weakness. I wanted so badly to be weak, vulnerable and sad; but I had a family that looked to me as a source of comfort and hope. They knew that I had faith in God, and they believed that my faith in Him was a lot stronger than theirs. I guess it was true in a sense, but I still fought so much to be strong in their face so that they wouldn't break. I had to solely depend on God in this time of my life because, to me, it was impossible to survive this tragedy. I had to be strong in the planning process of her burial. I had to gain the strength to see my mother lying on her back at the viewing and then turn around and say my last goodbye at her funeral. It was the toughest process I had ever walked through.

God truly helped me remain strong and composed during the whole process of getting ready to prepare her for her resting place. The memorial service for my mom was beautiful. As me and my family made our entrance inside the sanctuary, I glanced and saw so many familiar faces that I hadn't seen in years. Everybody that loved and adored my mother showed their respects; and I thought to myself: My mom was truly one of a kind; she was loved. This gave me a sense of peace. I even saw some of my school friends in the audience, and then that's when I really knew that people cared about me. My mom was blessed to have such an amazing homegoing service. Our church family came and supported me, even our pastor, who was kind enough to give the eulogy.

The eye of the storm where there is no rain, wind or lightning was the fact that God was with me. My church family held me up. And the reassurance that my mother gave her life to the Lord a year prior was confirmation to me that her soul was free. Her life was not easy; but now she can be free from every regret, every mistake and every burden that inflicted her emotionally, physically and financially. My hope was that I knew I would surely see her again and that until then, I have to let her live through me in everything that I do because I knew that she would only want me and my siblings to remain strong.

Months after my mother's passing, my life started to get extremely challenging, as my grades began to decline due to the depression and the grief I was enduring. Having faith does not make feelings of suffering and depression absent. Sometimes it can even amplify them because your life is not like what you believe it to be and greatly contradicts your future.

I would attend classes and find myself crying nonstop as I sat at my desk trying to complete my last year of 8th grade. It was hard for me to focus because every time I closed my eyes, I would see her beautiful face. Every time I would lay my head on my desk and tune everyone out, I would hear her soft-spoken voice. It was so bad for me. My teachers saw the pain I had endured and would allow me to step outside the classroom so that I could let out my tears of grief. They had become very compassionate towards me, seeking to understand what I was facing. They allowed me to take things easy as I got through the last couple of weeks of school before graduation. I appreciated their kind gestures, but it was so difficult for me that I would call my eldest brother on the phone so that he would pick me up from school.

I felt so alone at school because nobody my age understood the death of a parent. I wanted so desperately to be with my family. I couldn't stand being at school. I was so caught up in the depression that my mother's death caused me that I wasn't even concerned if I would graduate or not because my focus was on the void that was missing in my heart and life. I just didn't care anymore about school or anything outside of what I was dealing with.

Her death affected my mental, my physical and emotional being. I started to have recurring thoughts of suicide. I started to believe that I wouldn't get through this loss. I didn't lose my faith in God, but I felt so helpless and broken. I lost my appetite to eat, which I started to lose a lot of weight to where it became a concerning matter. I had picked up my old bad attitudes that I once had when I was younger. I became very antisocial and irritable. I became all these things because I didn't know how to get through my mom's death.

Though these behaviors were natural for a child who had just lost her mother, I then began to feel like these behaviors would become the death of me. So, I quickly sought counseling at my school to ensure that I wouldn't lose who I was because of the grief I was suffering from. And surely counseling was the greatest decision I had made during this time. It was as though the counselor knew just what to tell me. He knew just how to handle me. It was just what I needed to get through school.

Attending counseling slowly helped to improve my behavior, and it restored my thrive to finish 8th grade. After I had completed my therapy sessions and graduated from that, the school dean called for me to come to his office. It scared me because I had no hope that I would graduate on time. In fact, I honestly didn't even think I would graduate because, yes, I wasn't as focused and, yes, I lost my mother. But the words of my grandmother came to my mind as I walked to his office. I heard so loudly "You're not gonna graduate middle school." Those words crippled my mind, almost causing me to faint because I had believed that, considering the struggle it was to even complete an assignment for school. I was convinced that the call to his office was confirmation of my grandmother's words.

Well, when I walked in the dean's office, he looked at me with a blank face and said, "Kyshawna, please have a seat. I have important information to tell you." As I sat down, my heart started pounding, my hands started sweating and my legs started shaking. The dean proceeded to tell me, "I have good news for you. You're graduating with the Class of 2009. Congratulations. As I can imagine, this has been a hard journey for you. I'm inspired by your strength, Kyshawna. You made it despite it all." I began to allow the tears to flood my face because the words of my grandmother had not come to pass. In fact, this proved that she was wrong.

At that moment, I felt my mother's presence so strong that I began to gain my joy back (slightly). I was happy that God proved every naysayer wrong and that I was breaking generational curses. I was proud of my determination and strength to get through. As I thought I wasn't doing much to get by because I was blind and caught up in my own sorrow, I had to be proud that I did what people said I couldn't because of their own beliefs and doubts. God proved to everyone that I could accomplish what they deemed impossible. I have to give all the credit to God because He sees and knows all, and He saw fit to grace me with the opportunity to graduate in the midst of my depression and pain.

From that day onward, I knew that I was capable of achieving anything regardless of what life threw at me. I knew in my heart that my mom was proud of me. I just wished my grandmother was as proud of me as my mom would have been. But sadly, she was embarrassed by her words because God proved her wrong. Interestingly though, she didn't even show up at my graduation, which hurt my feelings; but I figured it was to be expected. My brother and the great man who took care of me in the form of a father showed up in support of my accomplishment, and it made my heart happy to see at least two familiar faces at my graduation.

I accepted what was and was proud that I didn't allow my agony to overshadow my success and my journey. I succeeded in the face of those who doubted my path. God has a funny way of proving people wrong, and I'll forever be grateful that I made it over that hurdle. My mother's death birthed in me an overachiever and a stronger fighter. I couldn't be happier that it did. I learned in these moments that I can now take these abilities and conquer anything life throws at me, and surely I did.

Undeniable Call

T hey say the last stage of dealing with any type of grief is acceptance. Even as it still hurts and you are still healing, you have to come to terms with your new reality without a certain person, place or even object. The truth is that you can grieve due to other aspects of your life other than the loss of a family or friend. You can also lament over lost friendships, opportunities, possessions and time. There will come several moments in your journey where you will muse and ponder on what life could have been for you, how things could have gone if someone treated you better or if someone did not pass away so soon and how your purpose and desires can either make certain people accept you or reject you.

While your purpose can be phenomenal, it also comes with a set of unwritten rules and criteria that will conflict with what you want and what others will want for you. Sacrifices must be made in order to walk in greatness; but the outcome is worth it, especially when you know it will help someone else heal.

Losing my mother caused me to collapse and just freeze in my mind. The next few seasons coping with this new normal was like waking up to a nightmare every day, hoping that I could one day sleep and my dreams of better would be a reality. Even though going to church for these last few years has helped me put the pieces of my identity together, my mom's passing shattered the mirror of my heart all over again; and a piece of me died along with her.

Feelings of rejection, abandonment and confusion would often plague me, for now I had neither of my parents to hold me, love me and tell me how precious and valuable I am. I literally ask myself often at this point who am I? What am I, and even why am I here? The absence of both of my biological parents increased the gap between me and what I knew and felt was my purpose.

When I initially became a Christian, a new set of desires and passions were acquired; and my time became occupied with many activities and events offered at my church. Serving on the choir, dance team and praying often in my own personal time would open my eyes to the possibility of being an official leader. All I knew at the time was that preaching was whenever the pastor or one of the ministers got up to the podium for a half hour or more, discussed a certain topic and then centered that topic around the Bible, while making it relatable to our present-day reality.

I knew being in ministry was a road less traveled and that you truly need to be drawn to it and not just want it because it looks glamorous; but I had to plow through all of my grievances and doubts before I could get to a place of accepting that this is the path that I just did not want to take, but was destined to take. This was something I could not rush into, and I needed time just to really gather myself again after the present circumstances I endured that distorted my vision for who I want and what I want in my life.

Feeling unqualified is an understatement. Even though I graduated middle school, I still wrestled with the whispers of my family and school teachers who swore that I would never be intelligent or worth anyone's time. When you have heard these curses spoken over you during your whole life, it takes quite some time to truly heal and recover from the wounds inflicted upon your psyche. I had immense fear and concern that I would fail greatly, that I would make a fool of myself and that everything I went through and suffered would literally be a distraction from people being able to receive me in that light.

Singing and dancing are not that easy either; but I thoroughly enjoyed them as my escapes and natural talents, for it also helped that singing and dancing was often done with a group of people performing alongside you so that you're not feeling like you were up there by yourself. Being a church leader was a different story, for you feel the weight of the world on your shoulders. Anything you do or say could literally pull someone towards the church or push them away.

Starting high school gave me a fresh start with new people, so I was able to develop a positive reputation compared to how everyone saw me in my previous schools. It felt good to belong and be accepted and popular by various classmates who considered me cool and fun to be around. But, I knew I could only hang out with them only so much just to make sure I never compromised my personal boundaries and convictions with certain customs and habits that many teenagers develop during these years.

I can count on my hand how many parties I attended. I was usually leaning off to the side and laughing at everyone else, especially if they were under the influence of smoking or drinking. I knew I could not and would never touch those things, so I would be around it without blatantly trying to get involved. Even though I knew the behaviors of my peers would conflict greatly with my newfound beliefs, I just wanted to be accepted and not have to endure anymore rejection and abandonment than I had already faced.

When you are of a certain religion, just saying the name of what and who you follow comes loaded with plenty of preconceived notions by everyone around you. Many knew I went to church, which was pretty normal and understandable; and it did not stop them from wanting to be around me. However, I knew that if I were to one day become a preacher, it would change everything. I could envision my classmates twisting their faces and not wanting to be around me anymore, making snarky comments like I am too holy for them or that I think I am better than them just because I choose not to smoke, drink or get involved in minor, reckless behaviors.

I certainly feared being ostracized and rejected, especially if I would have to endure it for a full four years in high school. I contemplated if I should just wait until I am an adult and just allow myself to live a little, not too reckless but just enough so that I can feel normal for just one moment in my life. I am crushed between the two walls of my own personal insecurities and fearing the opinions of everyone around me. Even when I knew the love from these said people would not always be genuine, I was more than willing to settle for tolerance.

I spent a full two years measuring the cost of this assignment, still praying and studying the scriptures as I allowed my mind and heart to be healed and placed back together. I often had to pray and ask the Lord why would He even consider me knowing everything I had been through. The answer that I would feel in my heart was that this mission is older than my circumstances and that I was always meant to be this way. I was meant to be in ministry all along, even before everything had happened to me growing up.

My past did not cancel or block my future, but rather solidified the fact that I survived everything I had endured up until now. I felt that these things prepared me to be an impact on others and that I will be used to give many people hope while resuscitating their dreams. I had to come to grips with the fact that I was created to never fit in, not in my family or amongst my peers. As a leader, I cannot afford to follow the crowd and everything I am told to do just to make others comfortable. I was meant to create a path that will lead others to the love of God.

I am also grateful that I was not rushed into something like this either, as my leaders were patient with my process. I began to study the different types of preachers and messengers found throughout the Bible's history. I saw their backgrounds, their family and personal dysfunctions, their fears and how God still loved them and desired to use them, promising that He would guide them and teach them directly how to spread His word to many.

I have already carried a lot on my shoulders with everything I was facing in my family and education, so they allowed me to cruise through this vocation while providing me with valuable resources. Many church leaders in the community caught wind of how much I served in church and how I was navigating a potential ministerial calling, so they provided me with all kinds of books, resources and even one-on-one training sessions surrounding how to carry yourself as a ministry leader, dissecting and properly communicating the scriptures and writing sermons. I was being molded into who God always meant for me to be since the day I was conceived, and I came to the point where I was ready to accept the cost.

When I saw the results of my singing, dancing, praying and encouraging others and how it caused many to accept God and to find healing and wholeness, I knew that this was non-negotiable, for the impact I would create would be priceless.

I remember the first day I spoke in front of a crowd of people. It was quite interesting and revealing. As I walked up to the podium, I began to get really excited to have been given this opportunity to share my heart in words. I felt excited because in that moment, I found a sense of purpose in the earth. The message that was prepared that day was something that I needed, as well as the people in the audience. My message was entitled "Do Not Allow Your Past to Dictate Your Future."

As I prepared this message, I was reminded of all the times I thought about how my past and current situations would determine if I would have a good future or not. I was wrong. Your past does not determine how your future will turn out because we do not know the future at hand. None of us know what tomorrow will bring. And having a set mind allowed me to hope for a great journey ahead.

I had to get the negative thoughts out of the way and manifest positive thoughts that would feed into my future self and life. I had to speak over my life in positive ways, as we know words have power and they have presence meaning. Whatever you speak and demand, it shall happen. That's a dangerous ability to have because we have the power to speak what we want to happen in our lives. Also, what we often think sometimes becomes our reality. So, it is important that we feed our mind positive thoughts and speak positive declarations over our lives.

I found this to be true because I am evidence that words have power and presence because my grandmother had always spoken negative words about me concerning my life and my mental inabilities. When she would speak negative words, it would make me believe that her words were true because I would start treating myself negatively. Gratefully, I came to my senses and gave those words back that she spoke over me. I said all this to say never let your past dictate where you are going in the future because only God knows the blueprint of our lives.

The first time I was ever asked to speak, I had feelings of nervousness because out of all people, I couldn't fathom why they chose me, why they chose the shy girl to stand in front of hundreds of people to share encouraging words. I guess they believed that I was capable of doing such a task.

As I prepared for my first message, I had no idea what I was doing. I didn't know where to start or what to talk about, and I had no idea how to communicate the message I had prepared. I remember feeling incapable of creating a message to speak to the people, which left me with feelings of frustration and irritation. It seemed that everything I wrote on paper made no sense to me. I just knew that the people wouldn't understand what I was talking about.

I stepped away from my paper and prayed for peace for this assignment. I knew that I was fighting with these feelings because what was in me was great and necessary. I gained the strength and courage to go back to my paper, and that's when I received the message "Do Not Allow Your Past to Dictate Your Future." I decided on that message because it was appropriate for where I was in my life. While exercising my gifts of singing, dancing and speaking, I still had thoughts that I wasn't going to be good enough to fulfil these things in the future. I was completely wrong.

After giving my first speech, I remember people coming up to me expressing how encouraged and blessed they were by my message. That left me with a little motivation to keep going. People would begin to tell me that my message really pulled them out of a horrible place mentally and emotionally and that they had hope and faith for their future. I then knew that this was something that I had been destined to do. Hearing all these different people tell me how impactful I was to them made me appreciate the frustrating moments I had experienced during the preparation of my message.

This had become a part of who I was. I began to always use my words to encourage and speak life into those that were around me. Every time I would talk with my friends, they would tell me things like "Kyshawna, you are always so encouraging. Every time we talk, it's as if you understand me." Hearing those words frequently really encouraged my heart. It encouraged me to keep fighting and believing in the lives of my friends and people that I'd run into on a daily basis. Encouraging and motivating people became one of my all-time favorite things to do.

I love to uplift people because I knew how it felt growing up and not having people speak positively into my life. I was giving people what I never received as a child, and it honestly made me feel like I had purpose; that if I encouraged people and loved people, then I have completed the assignment on my life.

Accepting who God had created and called me to be was easy because I loved who I was becoming. Being the overlooked and worthless child to being the sought after and valued child changed my perspective on life.

A Repeated Cycle

I t has been a proven scientific fact that you can work better and think clearer in a clean and organized space. More times than not, your surroundings or the organization of your room and living space can both influence and reflect the state of your mind. The more the clutter on the outside, the more discombobulated your thoughts may be. Too many stimuli can drive you crazy and can cause all kinds of emotional and spiritual turmoil.

Many times, people do not take the time to consider how their words, actions and habits can disturb your peace and rock you deep to your core. When you were younger, or at any age, as a matter of fact, you always hoped that your dreams and aspirations would, by virtue, demand a certain level of joy, respect and support but only to find out the harsh reality that life is not always going to be like that.

Unfortunately, your dreams may cause those you least expect to despise you, even amongst your circle of family and friends. It irritates several of them for reasons such as there is no room for them in your plans. Relationships need healthy boundaries and readjustments so that you can pursue your passions. And plainly, it irritates them that your positive goals go against the failure and negative expectations that they have conjured in their mind concerning you. The moons of bitterness, hatred, jealousy and rejection pull the waves over you and will attempt to make you sink into the cold-hearted standards prepared for you.

The unfortunate dysfunctional dynamics of my household were at an all-time high. Many of my family members still saw the hopeless and helpless little girl I used to be, and their minds were made up concerning my life and future. Even though I made it through elementary school and graduated middle school, nothing could ever move the mountains in their mind that saw me as a failure and a disappointment.

They started going to church with me for a season. But by this point in time, they still had hardened their hearts towards what God was doing in my life. Their insults wounded me deeply, and I could not find affirmation or refuge in them. Every time I shared my dreams, I was told to be realistic with my limits, to succumb to the natural statistic that there was no way I would ever recover or break out of my chains. Nothing I would ever say or do would ever make any of them proud of me, especially my grandmother.

In spite of how much I achieved in leadership at church and in education, defying the odds with my learning struggles and IEP (Individualized Education Program), I still had to come home every day to my grandmother who still had the same opinions about me from the day I was born. My petals were cut off, and I felt like my butterfly wings were cut off every time something cold was uttered from her lips, reminding me of how much of a burden I was to her and how she looked forward to finally getting me out of her house.

She would often compare me to my brothers and peers at school who were no longer my friends and would belittle me because of my subpar performance while they excelled. It took everything in me to barely pass my classes and complete high school with everything going on in my mind and heart. She stated that my chances for continuing my education at a college were slim because I was not proficient or advanced in any area of study, especially in math and science.

Since high school was almost over, I was reminded constantly that whether I graduated high school or not, I would have to get out of her house by the time I was 18 years old, for my adoption funding from the government would run out by then. It left me feeling confused and worried. I had to constantly think of why she would want something like this to happen. I would be confused because at the time, we had several different people living with us and never once did she charge them rent. As a matter of fact, she never told my brothers that they had to leave; and we were all in the same situation.

I remember feeling worried to the core of my stomach when my grandmother would constantly tell me that soon I would have to leave her house. I hated feeling like I was going to be asked to leave at any moment because my grandmother was unpredictable. She treated you how she wanted and when she wanted, and that was unfair. I thought to myself how could someone be this evil to a little girl who's trying her best to live and do the right things.

I was the different child in the house because I wasn't involved in the behaviors of everyone else: The drugs, the violence, the perversions. I would think "What if I was like these people? Would she then treat me differently?" I would be tempted with the thoughts of doing what everyone else was doing. However, something on the inside of me would tell me that I was far greater than becoming a carbon copy just to be accepted and loved by my grandmother.

My grandmother would always have me and my little brother take the bus to school because she had to get to work in the mornings. I'd have to say that riding the bus was good for me because I was able to get away from her and ride the bus with my brother. My first initial thought when my grandma told me that I had to ride the bus was anger because I couldn't understand why she would put us on the bus at this young age. But it turned out to teach me what responsibility was, and I handled it well.

In fact, this was one of the greatest decisions she made for my brother and me because before school started, I could get a good laugh or two in. There were many memories created for me on the bus. I met a lot of people that I just clicked with immediately. I would talk, sing, laugh and enjoy the 30-minute ride to school every day with the other students that I would meet. I remember feeling embarrassed the first couple days of catching the public city bus because I didn't think other kids were on the bus. I didn't want to be made fun of for being the kid whose parents didn't care much for because I was on the bus. As you can see, I was wrong.

During this time, drug addicts and drug dealers were allowed to come in and out of my house. Strippers could move in and also conduct their business as well. But yet, my grandmother's main concern was me getting out soon. I could barely study for school or pray and prepare for church events due to how crowded, congested and chaotic my house was. This had been the norm of my entire childhood and teen years; but the climax of calamity in this toxic environment was taking its toll on me in every way possible.

On top of all of this, my grandmother allowed a young man to move in and stay, being well aware of my negative history with him. The man who molested me repeatedly when I was 11 now lived with us. I not only had to deal with the curses of my grandmother's words, but now I had to come home to the threats and abuse of this offender daily.

The house was so crowded that I had to study in the kitchen, and he always came around me and never gave me room to breathe.

He happened to be skilled in math and science, so he kind of forced his help on me because I had no one else I could ask. However, during the times I was trying to do my work, he would call himself assisting me. He would just stare at me up and down and compliment me, unfortunately entitling himself like I owed him a favor even though he had taken so much of my peace and stability.

Every single night, he would knock on my door asking to come in. I would never respond, silently praying he would go away. More times than not, he would get tired of knocking and still come in and continually press upon me, and there was nothing I could do to fight him off. I hated him so much and was infuriated that my family would allow this to happen to me and not care.

When I was a child and up until now, every time I would tell my grandmother, she would silence me and deny it, saying I am just crying for attention. I was drowning in an ocean with a ceiling and could not escape, being held down by fear, frustration and feeling forsaken by everyone alive and dead. I already had my own battles to fight on the inside, and these outside occurrences only added more unnecessary anguish and agony. It was in moments like these that I wondered if my life was ever going to get better with all my personal growth or that I would be dragged back down to square one and would never escape.

How could I possibly be successful in school with all of this toxicity and trauma killing me slowly every single day? The walls closed in on me so much that I no longer could think about the class or lesson in front of me. Being a junior in high school was so devastating because my academic performance reached an all-time low. Not having that many friends, no safe environment and seemingly no hope at the moment, the rug of finding refuge was pulled from me abruptly. I am lost in my loneliness once again. I would be so overwhelmed with the whispers of my family and former friends running rampant in my head that it made my eardrums ring.

I would frequently have to leave in the middle of class and just pace back and forth outside. I am in so many cages all at once, and all I can do is scream and cry about everything. My brokenness is at an all-time high, and I am trying so hard to live the life I feel I was called to as a Christian leader; but it seemed impossible. The only thing I knew to do was to pray and ask God to help me through all of this, but it just would not let up.

Being constantly moody, tired, depressed, aggravated and just over everything, the only grace I had in this season were teachers who gave me multiple chances to pass exams and assignments and would create opportunities for me to receive extra credit.

On top of everything that was happening to me and around me, the aspect that made everything different was my spiritual sensitivity. As a believer, you grow in the Lord to the point that you are able to see beneath the surface of so many situations and people. I can literally see the impure motives and agendas of everyone in my household, school and on the school and city buses, for I was never offered a ride to school. I could not turn off what my spiritual eyes would see, and it would drive me crazy.

My house was filled with so much negative spiritual energy from the drugs, drinking, prostitution and perversion, that I could barely sleep and would have to pray and worship through the night just to keep from going insane. I had a front row seat to the class of spiritual warfare. And even though my normal grades were suffering, I was gaining clarity and experience spiritually that you could never learn in a classroom. Growing in prayer was truly painful, for I often found myself interceding for the same people who hurt me and betrayed me, asking God to touch their hearts and make them confront the darkness that corrupted them and caused them to inflict damage on everyone they come in contact with.

This season is where I learned the road to purpose is not always pretty. Just like mud and manure are needed for flowers and fruit to flourish, so is the messiness of my life, even in the midst of failure and frustration. I could not see how any of this would ever let up or that I would overcome this wall blocking my path. Just the fact that my teachers gave me room to pass and make it through and that I was still able to somehow grow in my spirituality in spite of all the darkness, I learned that even though the quote says "survival of the fittest," it should be survival of the favored!

I know you're probably wondering how in the world did she go through all this and still remain faithful to her life's call and duty? Well, I have to give honor where honor is due. God himself ensured me that I was different from people, that my strength doesn't come from my own ability but from Him.

Though my journey living in this household was tough, I still was aware that I had a far greater calling on my life. And if I was to bend and fold at the chaos my life was in, then I would not be able to fully walk out and be who God wanted me to be. I would wipe my tears, pray and ask God for strength for the journey, strength to get through what was seemingly impossible to most. And He did just that.

Yes, my heart was broken; but I knew in my mind that I couldn't give up because my life was attached to people who needed to see me survive so that they could survive as well. It was almost as if people needed my survival so that they could gain from it and not give up in their own personal life. Yes, it was hard; but thriving and fighting off the chaos was worth it. I still found the strength to encourage and push my friends and those who were in need of help. My life still had meaning, and I wasn't going to allow my family to get in the way of me walking in my God-given call.

Breaking The Curse

T he process of a seed becoming a blade of grass, a flower or a tree has always been ironic and inspiring. A seed for flowers and fruit can be so small and seem insignificant and is often discarded in the trash. It is often looked at as a distraction to the consumer biting into the fruit. Too many times we are guilty of forgetting that the fruit we hold is the result of seeds that were not thrown in the trash but sown in the ground. Even this process of planting can seem counterproductive, for dropping it into the soil can have its fair share of risks and disadvantages.

Not every seed grows due to either being in the wrong soil or being consumed by worms or birds. The ones that are fortunate enough to grow go through being buried deep in the ground, covered in mud, scorched by the heat of the sun and drenched by the pouring rain. Some farmers and planters go as far as to fertilize the soil and seeds with manure, which is mixed with the waste of cows. Something so deplorable actually fosters the development of transforming a seed into its full and final potential.

Seeds will never take their true form and identity until they are buried and broken open by all the circumstances the seeds must endure. And just like these seeds, we too experience growth and tapping into our potential, not just from the blessings but also from the brokenness of our lives. Even to the point that if we are forgotten in the soil and then covered in cement, we still break through the concrete and become evidence that our delicate desires for light will break us out of the darkness plowed upon us by the trials and tribulations of life.

I cried out of fear and frustration for many days, praying for the noise to cease and for a mind to work and achieve what has been deemed impossible by everyone around me. My only option was to fight for my future, no matter how much the quicksand tried to make me sink into hopelessness. By the latter half of my senior year of high school, my grades improved drastically. I finally managed to not just pass but excel with A's and B's, which I had not done in a long time due to the grief of losing my mother and the trauma I endured daily from verbal, emotional, physical and sexual abuse. This was indeed beyond difficult, but one thing it was not was impossible.

From the months of March to June of 2013, I plowed through every single deadline, making sure my assignments were on time, even if I had to stay up several nights in a row to do so. I shoved everything and everyone else in the recesses of my mind and kept in front of my eyes the vision of graduation and receiving my diploma, something many told me I would never have during the whole course of my childhood and adolescence.

As I am near the end of the school year, my grades were certain; and qualifying to graduate was already guaranteed. However, I had a new major concern that would begin to weigh on my heart. Would I even be able to enjoy all the festivities and celebrations to commemorate this moment that I worked long and hard for? Everything costs in order to celebrate graduation, including senior photos, a cap and gown, a class ring, getting clothes and makeup for prom and the tickets for graduation.

I had absolutely nothing to cover any of these expenses, and my family could not and would not help me due to how tight everything was financially for them. I would not have expected them to cover all of it either. Even half or a portion of the costs was treated like a burden to them, even though it was for a great cause of being able to reach a milestone that so many do not get to enjoy due to dropping out, addiction or even getting involved in gangs and selling drugs. There was no one I could turn to for help, so I was left to come up with the money all by myself.

I only had one option that I could utilize, which was asking Child Services in my area for financial assistance so that I could get everything I need to celebrate my victory. I found out that part of being a foster child included having access to funds and resources for when graduation comes around so that you can be able to move forward in your journey into adulthood. All I could do was pray for this provision and then step out on faith and journey to the Child Services building in my neighborhood.

I took the bus one day, holding onto my birth certificate, Social Security card, my faith and the desire to enjoy this period of my life. I got off at my stop and walked up to the building with a conflicted confidence, knowing this was the only way. The lady I met with was truly kind and compassionate, as she asked me what I had arrived to talk about. I expressed how I needed help so that I could afford the essentials for my high school graduation, to which she empathetically replied, "You came to the right place at the right time!" After my paperwork and documents were verified, I was given the exact amount of money that I needed to cover every single one of my expenses. What I needed was waiting for me all along.

I was able to purchase my cap and gown, take my senior photos, get a dress, get makeup and get my hair done for my senior prom. And ultimately, on June 8, 2013, I walked across the stage and graduated with my high school diploma. I was adorned in achievement and reached a major goal in my life against all odds. I did not have the finances, stability or support that I needed from my family; but I was still provided for and taken care of in such miraculous ways, even from people who barely knew me, like the woman at the Child Services Center. Sometimes the love and support you are looking from will come from complete strangers who will change your life in a matter of moments.

By now, I am still not completely out of the mud of my history; but I am starting to crack through the concrete of every doubt and curse I've wrestled with since the day I was conceived. It was becoming clear to me that I am intelligent, powerful and have the potential to accomplish anything I desire to do. Even when no one else believed in me, I struggled periodically to believe in myself. What helped me turn the tassel of my past was knowing that I have a Father in Heaven who believes in me and knows what I am capable of; and I can rest in that assurance whenever my own faith in myself falls short.

I wanted to go to college but could not go right away until I gathered some funds, so I started working at the TJ Maxx in my area where I would have to take the bus too. During this period of my life, there was barely any food in the house; and I was only able to eat if I bought my own food. In addition to that, the water would act up; and the bills would go unpaid. So, I had to make sure I took care of myself and sometimes hopefully have enough money to get some food for the rest of my family. I worked hard and diligently so that I could live somewhat comfortably.

In addition to all of this, my grandmother was still threatening me daily that since I was now 18, I was no longer under the foster system and that it meant she would not be able or willing to take care of me anymore. I figured that putting myself in school and working hard would show that I am working towards being independent enough to one day stand on my own.

While in my senior year in high school, I also learned that the state government assists children who are former foster children to go to college. I went through the process to gain the assistance that I needed to ensure I could attend college. So, here I am. I started my first attempt at college, thinking I was truly ready and prepared for the challenges that would be presented to me. Unfortunately, I would learn how all of my wounds and running on a survival mentality would squander my plans for being in school. I found myself overwhelmed with the amount of workload I had to plow through, the commute to and from college, the level of work and study for class and working full-time so that I could pay for my own food, clothes and school books. It was hard on me because I am internally battling, as well as fighting to stay afloat.

My emotional baggage was no help, not realizing until now how much bitterness and unforgiveness I was carrying in my heart. It felt truly unfair that I had to put myself through college and that things at my house never became stable like I needed them to be. I had dealt with failure before, so I would rather bow out gracefully than be put to shame.

So, with this, I dropped out of community college before the grades could become permanent. I came to the conclusion that this is not for me. Having graduated high school was more than I thought I could ever accomplish, and I barely made it through. There was no need for me to be in school anymore. I would now be working two jobs to support myself, believing I can do this until times got better or until I could receive some kind of raise or promotion.

While going through the whole threat of being kicked out, I reached out to Child Services to see if they could help me with possible housing. I learned that they helped foster kids with that as well. The same lady who helped me with my senior expenses directed me to the individuals that would assist me with this matter. I was led to believe that I had the possibility of receiving help, so I filled out housing applications every single day.

I would submit applications and check them all the time. I received calls back just to find out that my applications were all denied. Every single application I filled out and submitted was denied. This left me feeling even more scared for my future. I already knew the day was coming soon that my grandmother would release me from her house. I didn't have much hope because everywhere I turned, nobody could get me into my own spot.

I did this for a full year after graduating high school, and I worked as hard as I could to keep myself afloat and to build up my independence, working full- time, applying for housing apps, seeking out help, etc. However, all of this was in vain because in the eyes of my family, the threats of being kicked out for so many years finally became a reality.

Abruptly on August 24, 2015, my grandmother told me, out of the blue, it was time for me to remove myself from her house. I tried my hardest to negotiate, that I could help pay the rent with my two checks, which only came out to $200. She stated that it would not be nearly enough to help her. It would be one thing if she had given me a few months' notice, even a few weeks of notice so that I could plan and prepare myself accordingly. It was absurd to me that my brothers, who were older than me, unemployed at the time and showed no work ethic or educational ambition, were not forced out by her; just me. It was bad enough that I felt like the black sheep in her eyes the whole time I lived with her, but this truly was the climax.

My grandmother gave me less than a week to leave her house. I used the little money that I had to go and buy boxes to place all of my belongings in. Once I had packed up my room, I would then spend this time being homeless and having to hop from house to house while still working and serving in the church. I would spend the night at various people's houses so that I would be able to shower and get dressed for work the very next day. I hated going through this because it was humiliating. I hated having to ask someone new every day if I could shower and sleep at their house. I was young and traveling from place to place with my hygiene items and clothes. I didn't want people seeing me in that light, but I had to come to grips that this was just my conclusion.

I would then truly learn that just because someone can help does not mean they will always be inclined to or desire to help you with pure intentions. I say that because there had come a time where I would spend the night at several different women ministers' houses with their families; and they would say things like "You can stay with us as long as you want, but you must sing or speak at our church."

When I first heard this from a family whom I adored and respected so highly, my stomach would turn upside down; and I thought to myself, "Did they just say that to me?" You may wonder if that was a good or a bad thing. Well, in my eyes, it was a bad statement to make towards an individual who's dealing with brokenness and turmoil. I thought how could these people offer me a place to stay but tell me (not ask me) that I MUST sing at their church?

There was never a moment where I was asked if I was okay. I was never asked if I needed an open heart so I could vent and let out what was in me. There was never a time that they sat me down and poured into me. It was always what I could do for them while I lived with them. It broke my heart to learn that just because people are in church does not mean they have your best interests at heart.

Sadly, because I had no other place to go, I stayed with this family for a while. It was nice while it lasted. I was able to get myself together and find ways to get on my feet. I lived under their household, so I did just what they instructed until they started to harass me about my money and my attendance at their church, which led them to become undeniably controlling to the point that since they couldn't control me, they asked me to leave. I had never experienced this type of betrayal from a church family before, and I thought that this was the end for me.

I gathered my belongings and went on my way with the same feelings I had leaving my grandmother's house. I went through this cycle of living from house to house, leaving me with absolutely no hope that my circumstances would change. The same issues just decided to choose a new mask to hide behind, and I would soon learn that these masks were more abundant than genuineness.

The Enemy's Devices of Control

Birds never force their hatchlings to overstay their time in the nest. As they grow, the less room there is for them to remain without suffocating everyone else in their proximity. There comes a moment where the mother no longer needs to chew the food and then give it to her hatchlings because they become able to take solid food on their own. Their wings only get stronger through training and risks, which is why the young birds will be thrust out of the nest so that they learn how to fly and become independent.

Any parent, guardian, mentor or leader who fails to give those under their covering and tutelage the space to grow and exercise the tools and practices they learned under them has failed. It has been said throughout many generations that a parent or leader should desire their children or followers to do better and go farther than them, for the strides they make and the feats they accomplish are considered a testament to their training. To muzzle someone's potential is to abort and destroy your own legacy. While we expect our role models to celebrate our victories and the maturity in our skills and gifts, unfortunately those with unchecked insecurities and underlying intimidations will change their hearts if they see we are just as far or even farther than them.

As I continue to finesse through this season of being homeless, living from house to house and working two jobs to take care of my personal needs, I was still attentive to the needs of the church I attended. The odds had been stacked against me multiple times in my life by now, but I always found peace and joy in worship and seeking God and being amongst a community of believers who invested into my growth as a Christian and a leader. I found enough power in my heart to continue my life's purpose through speaking and singing, singing in spite of everything I faced, for it created wisdom, insight and fortified my relationship with God. I understood that nothing I went through would separate me from His love and that His hand would keep me from falling into despair.

My speaking engagements were flourishing like a flower in fertilized soil; and the healing and freedom that would come from the many churches, communities and children I would speak to was a great reward in itself. By now, I have been speaking for four years, since the age of 15. So, while I am not an expert or seasoned at this gift, I have gained some solid hands-on experience on how to navigate the world of impactful speaking.

Opportunities and platforms would begin to open up to me that I would have never imagined, and I would be traveling all through California and several other states to spread hope and encouragement. It was a beautiful, temporary escape from my personal woes. This gave me the healing and motivation to keep pushing towards my future. While I was not certain about the other areas of my life, like my career and education, I was certain that I could walk in ministry for the rest of my life. This was one of the only areas of stability and serenity that I had left to hold onto, and I was so certain that no one could take this away from me, especially because people in the church are expected to be loving and supportive.

However, I would begin to understand that even some of their love can turn into loathing, not because I did anything wrong, but because I was just being who God created me to be. Jealousy, envy and manipulation are old enemies for me that I fought daily in my family and amongst my peers in school. So, it was nothing new to me at all. I just never expected that those same evils could exist in the house of worship and come from leaders I had looked up to. To my dismay, some of the ones who I loved dearly in the church would show a new face.

It would be an honor when pastors and churches asked me to come preach or sing for their events. But out of honor and respect for my leaders, I would always pray to make sure the invitation was acceptable; and I would ask my pastor if I could accept it, for I would be representing my church, my leader and everyone who taught and trained me.

More times than not, my leaders would release me to minister elsewhere when requested; but there were a handful of invitations that I could not bring myself to receive. I would sense the impure motives of some of the places I would go to or consider walking through, knowing that their hearts were not towards God no matter what kind of title they had. It would not be about blessing the lives of their members or reaching new souls to receive the Lord's love; but, unfortunately, it was just to gain clout and have an influx of visitors and new members just so the offering plate could have more money.

Many would extend their doors to me not just to give me a chance to let God save someone's life through me, but rather to use up my power and preparation for what they lacked in study time and personal devotion to the God they say they worship. It was a dollar sign more than a gift; and this showed me that every rose has thorns, even the roses of the Kingdom.

Even in the midst of homelessness, some would try to use that weakness as an attempt to control me and persuade me to fulfill their agenda with my gift. Most of these leaders had families and houses with an extra guest room, and I reached out to some of them to ask if I could stay until I got myself together. Some would even offer it to me before I could ask.

The other issue that would present itself was a selfish bargain in exchange for having a place to sleep. I was told many times by various pastors that if I were to stay with their families, I would be required to leave my church, join their church and serve mainly for them. Their pride would not let them allow me to stay without them getting something in return, which is something that angered me to my core because of how I was used to this behavior from my grandmother and any other person that attempted to take advantage of me financially, emotionally, spiritually or sexually.

I would not bow down to the compromise that hid behind the stage and the microphone that you only get to see if you ever have the opportunity to be a leader in any field, both in the church and the secular field.

As more doors would open for me, the more the heart of my second pastor begins to turn cold and indifferent towards my growth and ever-increasing influence. It would start out with denials of certain invitations becoming more frequent than permissions to travel around the state and country. One day, it would get to the point where I was forbidden from preaching, singing or even visiting any other church.

Jealousy has a stench, and it was reeking in a place I never expected it to come from. The fake excuses were absurd and included reasons like people will take advantage of me, I was all of a sudden not ready and even that God never truly called me at all and that people were just giving me a chance just because I was young and sounded good. They literally took back everything good they said about me and my gift when I first started and now tried to force me to be on house arrest, if that is even a thing in the church.

They were happy for me as long as I stayed on their level. They became almost furious that I had only been in ministry for four years and went across the state and country when they have not placed their feet outside of the county.

Having the wisdom and discernment to navigate these pitfalls would cultivate the character of my calling and make me that much more valuable and integral as a woman and as a leader in my community. Maturing fast due to the life I lived prior to the church really helped me see how to walk on thin ice without cracking it and falling into the various traps set for me and other young preachers like me.

Since we are young, a lot of people will mistake our age for naivety and assume that we will automatically believe any and everything they tell us. They think our minds will tell us that we can trust them fully and that we will comply with their commands and instructions just because of the title in front of their name. In the various areas of your life, you can never take anything or anyone at face value. This is not an excuse or permission to have trust issues, but rather a warning to always read between the lines and to trust your heart and even ask a multitude of trustworthy friends and loved ones who can help you recognize the motives of others who want access to you.

Even though these various leaders showed me hatred and jealousy, I couldn't allow their actions to paralyze me and cause me to partake in their behaviors of hatred and bitterness. Instead, I humbled myself and continued to show love and appreciation towards these individuals. Because in their demise, what they were doing to me was actually building my character. I learned that just because they had the "power" to keep me from going places to speak and visit, they weren't stopping God from making ways and openings for me.

In spite of their control, God did move in my life. He still allowed me to be a voice for the voiceless. He still allowed me to impact lives through what everyone knows as social media. I used my social media platforms to spread positivity and hope to people who needed it, though I wasn't allowed to step in front of a building. I navigated my way through social media, and it did me justice. I had always been passionate about making a difference in the people's lives regardless of what my current situation looked like. I knew it was just fuel to make me much more effective to people who needed a change.

In spite of the constant hindrances of my leaders at the time, I still did what God instructed me to do and that was to remain faithful to His assignment on my life while still honoring leadership. It had all worked out in my favor; and, in the back of my mind, I knew that I was unstoppable and undefeatable. God will always have the last say concerning your life.

So, please, never allow the fear of others concerning your purpose stop you from fulfilling your God-given mandate. You are assigned to people who need everything you have to offer. And if you stay bound by the negative tactics and controls of man, you will never succeed or reach your highest potential. Always remain respectful; but never stay under the control of the devil because if you do, you will never be who you were predestined to be.

God's Mandate

You are not called to fit into everyone's space, for what is their comfort can become your cage. I am reminded of those blocks as a child where you would fit the right shapes with the right molds, and it is impossible for a triangle to fit into a circle mold or for a square to fit into a triangle mold. Every true leader will come to a crossroad in their life when they realize that they cannot afford to camouflage their calling to a purpose that outweighs their present pleasures.

Stepping out on a dream will cost you money, time and definitely friends. There will be many moments where you feel completely alone. But before any architect can install a light or build a city in the middle of a forest, they must be willing to embrace the wilderness and the isolation that comes with being a builder. When you pay close attention to your triumphs and your trauma, you will see how every single one of them has prepared you for your destiny, the path that no other man or woman could ever walk out for you.

I refused to give into the slavery disguised as submission and obedience, so I had no choice but to walk away from my church. This is where I spent the last eight years of my life, filled with some of my greatest victories and deepest sorrows. I discovered deeper spiritual gifts. They helped me through the process of my mother's death, and they originally invested into my calling as an inspirational leader. This was supposed to be my safe place and one of the only places where I could fully be myself and have peace.

It shattered my heart how the leadership betrayed me and attempted to muzzle me and use up all my energy for their own agendas. It was time for me to spread my wings, even when I had no idea whether or not I was ready yet. All I knew was my purpose could not afford to be contained or restricted by anyone, even if it means I have to walk alone.

Without having the outlet of a place to worship, the realities of being homeless would throb even more than usual due to it staring me in the face daily. I lost count of the various houses I stayed at, even if it was for one night, the shelters and the many nights I would sleep in and out of people's homes.

I was reminded of what God told me when I lost my

mother that even when I felt like I was alone, He was still with me. I could not allow the lack of a leader or a church home keep me from trusting Him and walking out the blueprint He had made for my life. I could not trust many pastors and leaders in my area due to their agendas and ulterior motives, so I walked alone with God for a season. And up until now, I have never heard Him more clearly. Without the voices of people who wanted to use me and those who were intimidated by me, I could be uninterrupted and have a clear mind and space to grow for just a season.

During this isolated time that I spent with my thoughts and God, I had begun to gain the desire to create a space for people like me to gather for a time of refreshment and inspiration. I remember how the idea for a special gathering or conference began to flood my dreams. Even though I was counted out by many, I still had a mind to be impactful and the desire to see people changed and freed from their past. I had a humble confidence that there is enough in my testimony and story for me to lead people into the right direction and to a better path for their lives. Up until now, I only was invited to various services and conferences but had never led one myself.

All I could do was go from the experiences I watched during my recent years and implement that into a context that would surely spark a light in my region. I would step out on obedience and launch my first ever gathering: ***The New Generation Experience.***

In the church world, it is often frowned upon to preach, lead or host any kind of service or conference without a pastor or church that you are accountable to and had permission from. I was willing to accept all those risks because I was used to being the outcast in every circle of my life.

During the journey leading up to the conference, I would have to go through some rough patches of forgiveness. Before I could move further in leadership and be an influencer for the youth of my community, I needed to make sure I began healing from the mental, emotional, financial and spiritual wounds inflicted upon me by word curses from family and peers, everyone who ever molested me and now from my former pastors and those in my community who shunned me and tried to take advantage of my gift. I had to make sure that I would speak to the people from a place of healing and not bleed on those who would attend.

The desired end result was not that people would be sympathetic and weep and leave depressed, but that they would be empowered and healed and receive a glimpse of the love of God from the parts of my life that I would be able to share with them.

In preparation of this conference, I had to come up with a budget, which turned out to be $5,000 in total to cover all expenses. I had to cover the cost of the venue, speakers, musicians and other guests who came to share their gifts, such as singing, poetry, dancing and acting. At the time, I was still working my two jobs while homeless; but I was so determined to create this time for people like myself to get away from the pain of their lives and enjoy a safe place of freedom. My determination allowed me to work countless hours at both jobs so that I could fund this mandate. Well, the time had come; and I was well over the amount that I needed to ensure that my event was fully funded.

The purpose of **The New Generation Experience** was to create a space where God could love on His people and for those who may or may not have church experience to be able to learn about Him, as well as address taboo topics that many churches shove under the rug.

In addition to myself, every speaker and panelist that I invited to be a part of this conference dealt with themes such as violence/drug addiction, many forms of abuse, such as emotional, physical, psychological, sexual abuse and much more from both a spiritual and statistical standpoint so that we could bring clarity and some sense of closure to those who have dealt with any or all of those areas.

It was not perfect, but the fact that I trusted God and believed in myself would continue to give me the grace to grow and make each consecutive conference and service better than the first. I had the confidence and power to go forth because I believed that I was mandated to have this gathering.

People came from all over the world to support the vision I had fulfilled, and they were extremely inspired by the faith that I displayed. There were people who came to the event that were broken, just as I was. They wanted to see a change in their lives, just as I did. They wanted to have people there that understood them, and they did. People were able to walk away from the conference with a new sense of identity and a new sense of purpose for their lives.

I was shocked to see the result of what faith did for these people.

Oftentimes we feel like going to church could be a waste of our time or going to any type of Christian event could be a waste of time because all they do is what? "Judge" and frown upon you. I know. I heard it all. This wasn't that type of event. This was an event like none other. This wasn't a Christian event. This was an event for people to come and get something that would make an everlasting impact on their lives.

I was never interested in the idea of just having church; but instead, I was interested in seeing people changed from the inside out. We sometimes live our lives thinking that we can change ourselves and thinking that we can escape our own sorrows by ourselves. Many times, we do that by partaking in drugs, alcohol and having countless sex partners. But in all actuality and truthfulness, these things only make us much more broken than we already were.

Don't worry. By this time in my life, I knew what it was like to be a young girl that had so many voids that so desperately needed to be filled. I still was fighting and struggling with the thoughts of not having both of my parents, still longing for parents, still longing to feel the love of a parent and still wanting to feel loved by my family and people in general. However, I didn't receive that.

Understand this: During this conference gathering, I was still homeless. I was still living from house to house. I was still hopeless concerning my living situation. I didn't think that I would make it, and I honestly just didn't care. I didn't care about what I was currently facing. All I cared about was the people gathering. I cared about seeing people free. I cared about seeing people changed. Because if I saw them changed, if I saw them free, then that meant to me that one day I could be free.

By walking in obedience and having this event, it proved to me that despite my sorrows, despite how hard my life was, I could still walk in greatness and I could still do great things.

I want to leave you with this: Never be afraid of looking yourself in the mirror. There is power in embracing where you are in life. I want to encourage you to embrace your flaws, but don't let them bury your perfections. Friend, embrace the calling on your life, embrace your undeniable gifts, embrace it all because soon one day you will be the answer to someone's prayer. You will be the reason they don't give up, the reason that their sense of purpose is revealed to them and the reason they can find their new sense of identity.

This is my story, and it is still being written right now as I speak. So, let my journey be a reminder to you that this is not the end for you. Where you or others have placed a period, change it into a coma because you are coming out of your chrysalis and preparing to soar.

I thank God for the chrysalis of the complications of my birth, being placed in foster care, the numerous experiences of abuse, perverted addictions, betrayal and lies, internal diagnosis, rejection/abandonment, losing both of my parents at an early age, homelessness, and poverty. Because of the trials and tests that cultivated my wings, I am now the butterfly that I was destined to be.

Don't close **DNA Exchange: The Pain Of A Foster Child, Volume 1** just yet. You've learned how I survived; but next time, you will learn about how I soared.

Final Words and Remarks

Thank you so much for taking this journey with me as I shared my story of overcoming adversity. Though my journey isn't over, let me remind you that everything that I have been through up until now has made me the woman that I am today; and there's nothing impossible to overcome. I hope that my story has inspired you to look at your story in a whole new perspective, knowing that no matter where you are in life or what you may be facing, you can overcome and beat all odds. Know that your story has nothing to do with you, but it has everything to do with those behind and ahead of you. Embrace the God- given journey that God has placed you on and be the light in someone else's life.

Never let someone else's idea of who or what they think you should be cause you to take up an identity that was never meant for you. You are who God says you are, not what someone else or a statistic labels you as. You are not obligated to measure up to anyone's expectations other than His because He, Himself, will help you reach them.

Remember that you are not your mistakes nor the mistakes of those who came before you. Those mistakes do not make up your identity. Maybe you have found yourself struggling with some of the same things found in my story due to being mishandled by abuse, word curses and traumas. Know that if you were mishandled, there is still hope on the other side; and it is now time to take your identity into your own hands because today your DNA has officially been Exchanged!

You are destined for greatness; and because you are destined for greatness, I encourage you to embrace your story and life's purpose because somebody somewhere is depending on your survival. As you close this book, I hope you gained clarity and closure for your own life and are now able to close the book of your past! As I get ready for Part 2 of my story, I now welcome you to the first page of your new life!

DNA EXCHANGE, VOLUME 2

To Be Continued…

WORDS OF LOVE & INSPIRATION

FROM

FRIENDS & FAMILY

<u>Alwayne Spencer</u>

Our relationship is rooted in Christ. I couldn't have asked for a better friend. From writing and singing original songs, preaching in our rooms, doing ministry together and going to gospel and R&B concerts, to walking down the "straight and narrow" path in high school and sharing laughs that only we understand, Kyshawna has been a friend indeed.

I remember during my 9th grade (her 10th grade) year, I'd walk by her in the F-Building, reading the Bible or praying with worship music blasting in her ears. I'd never pass her without first saying "Hello" or "Good Morning." I never knew a simple gesture at the start of the day could develop into such a fruitful friendship. It started one morning when the 1st period bell rang. I walked out of the F-Building for my first class, and my heart burned with compassion. For some odd reason, I decided to turn around. When I did, I saw her with tears in her eyes, and I heard her talking to God. That moment stayed with me forever.

As we grew closer during Spanish class and eventually became best friends, the humility, hilarity and courage she displayed pushed me to manifest God's purpose in my life through the art of obedience and authenticity. Her bravery continues to inspire me to be the best version of myself each day. I'm grateful for every hard conversation and moment of frustration that we share.

Through every accomplishment and setback, she has been there to encourage me. I think the greatest impact she has on my life is her testimony. Being able to witness how she lives it as it unfolds and evolves leaves me in a constant state of wonder. She has not folded to any of the pressures life has dealt because she chooses to endure. That's powerful to me.

The burden for humanity that she carries is intense. If a conversation was never held and we decided to sit in silence, her life and resilience would be the only words needed to change my perspective on destiny.

Kyshawna, you are such a gift to this world. Thank you

for following your heart and telling your story. This nation, amongst others, will be forever changed because of it.

Senoia Ortiz

Five years ago, I was diagnosed with major depression. I was struggling with suicidal thoughts due to being abused at home. I had nowhere else to go and no one I could turn to because I didn't trust anyone. It wasn't until later that year in April of 2015 that I attended the "Alive and Well" gospel concert when God allowed Kyshawna to come into my life. Since that day, she has made a huge impact on my life.

It is because of Kyshawna's Testimony, transparency, consistency and authenticity that I did not give up on life, myself and, most of all, God. Throughout this time, she has encouraged me, counseled me and helped me to fly. Kyshawna has taken me under her wing as a sister and did not give up on me. Even when I felt like I couldn't make it through, she would pray and minister to me. Her testimony itself has helped me to make it through the obstacles I was facing in my life and at home. I was able to find my voice with her sisterly love, worship and obedience to God. It has made a difference in my life because it has pushed me closer to God.

Wandjell Reneice Browning

I don't meet many people who pique my interest on social media, at least not enough that I want to befriend them, add them on other social media platforms, exchange personal stories and eventually fly across the country to support their life-changing projects. However, with Kyshawna, it was so different, so very easy to become friends. It was almost like we just knew the character of each other, and we trusted that gut feeling of "this person will be in my life forever."

When she finally told me about her book that she was writing, it came to me as a no-brainer because of the many obstacles she overcame. However, I was so excited! I was so inspired by someone who knew that it was only God's hand that helped her reach the level of success she had already obtained, but to continue to elevate is beautiful to see.

I've always told Kyshawna that she was going to shake the nation; and I'm just so blessed, privileged, really, to witness it. The DNA Exchange is going to change so many lives, and I'm here for it.

Founder and Executive Director of The Freedom Child Foundation

<u>Leina Saikali Willis</u>

Kyshawna is a light in my life. When I met her, I was her college counselor and she was my student; but she has also always been my teacher. She is a beacon of the amazing resilience and power of the human spirit. I have always believed that a person's reactions to events in their life are more important than the events themselves, because our reactions are what determine our outcomes. Kyshawna is a living embodiment of that.

She continues to inspire and motivate me by how she has turned her darkest moments into sources of light, but she doesn't stop there. Through humility and kindness, she reaches her hand out to those around her and pulls them into the light with her. She exemplifies how someone can use their difficulties to fuel good and kindness in the world. Through my darkest days, I just think of Kyshawna...her tenacity and drive to be great, her humility and kindness to help others and her spirit and resolve to bring good into the world... and I am taken out of my darkness and back into the light. From that first day she walked into my office, she has changed my life.

Citrus College, EOPS Counselor

Luana Coberg

When I first started my job at Jovenes, Inc., I never expected to have been impacted the way I was. I work with many youths at Jovenes, but there was one who I had the pleasure of befriending: Kyshawna Johnson. I first heard of Kyshawna through a video she made for Jovenes, where she shared her story, how/why she experienced homelessness and how she worked on overcoming that obstacle.

When I finally met her, she was just as incredible, if not more, than what the video portrayed. When I first watched the video, I cried out of sadness. Now when I watch the video, I cry out of proudness. I am so proud that even though she suffered through unfortunate life events, Kyshawna fought, worked her *ss off and owned her story.

Although she couldn't change her past, Kyshawna knew she could change how she perceived it and she could change her future. That mentality is exactly what made me admire her, be inspired by her, and what makes her so incredibly special to me.

She taught me that no matter what happens to you, if you make peace and are transparent with those events, then those negative events become life lessons. Those events become accomplishments, not failures. Those events have the opportunity to make you stronger (if you allow them to). Kyshawna inspired me to carry those messages in my heart, which I will continue to use over and over again as a tool to grow and become a better person.

Kelsee Viano

Kyshawna Johnson is one of the most inspirational women I have ever met. Her story, resilience and character has fundamentally changed my life. Through her willingness to share her most difficult experiences, Kyshawna delivers a message that has encouraged me and countless others to live a more transparent life in order to find our God-given purpose.

This book is for anyone that has struggled or faced doubt. Through Kyshawna's words, you will find not only a friend, but courage to walk unafraid towards your own future. May her words and experiences bring you strength so that you can also transform your life.

Foundation & Corporate Grants Manager

Eric Hubbard

Kyshawna is an inspiring example of what it takes to persist and succeed in the face of tremendous odds. Her story always reminds me that personal transformation is possible and that, with resilience, no goal is unachievable.

By surviving the foster care system and overcoming homelessness, Kyshawna has demonstrated that someone can change their situation in life, especially when they seek and find a supportive network. Kyshawna is an amazing storyteller who is able to bring you into the disheartening and unfair moments she has experienced, but still leave you with hope and faith. She is driven by the idea that she has survived so many hardships so that she has the opportunity to share her life so that others will be able to overcome the challenges they are facing.

Kyshawna's story is not yet finished--her future will allow her to continue to grow as a role model and empower those who will follow in her footsteps.

Director of Development & Strategic Partnerships. Jovenes, Inc.

Dwanaya Collins

Life is a crazy, beautiful rollercoaster ride...and sometimes the "crazy" part can be detrimental for many of us. Not for this one. Not for her. I've witnessed this young woman's growth at close range over the years, and it's nothing short of glorious. Kyshawna has endured and triumphed through circumstances and situations that have completely plateaued others in her generation. In response to contradiction, she worships. In the face of rejection, her heart remains pure, both toward the Lord and towards His people.

As a trailblazer, she burns for the liberation of her generation. That same fire leaves behind a unique path for those who will follow. If anyone's life depicts the very hand of God, it is hers. She's not only a source of inspiration for me, not only a friend, but she is a sister in every sense of the word. I bless God for seeing fit to cross our paths in this life and for gifting us both with a lifetime connection.

Joshua De Sousa

I have been following Kyshawna Johnson's life and ministry for at least seven long years now; and even from afar, I was truly taken aback by her passion and fire for the Kingdom of God and her generation. I honestly had no idea that the Lord would even allow me to be this close to her as a friend and little brother, and it is an honor and privilege that I do not take lightly.

I do not remember exactly when we became friends, but I remember how humble I felt once that was established whenever she actually started talking to me! She is down-to-earth and very approachable and never loses sight of her identity and individuality in the face of her ever-growing influence. Kyshawna is extremely loving, supportive and will always look out for you and encourage you when you need it the most.

I am so grateful to God for my big sister's life and love because not only is she a friend to us, but she is definitely a friend of God. His power, glory and love shine through everything she says and puts her hand towards. I can truly say that her journey makes her a true role model, inspiration and a worthy worshipper, warrior and wielder of God's word!

Brittany Lenore

I met Kyshawna over two years ago through a mutual acquaintance at the time. When I met Kyshawna, I thought to myself this young lady reminds me of myself. She was so vibrant, beautiful, funny and always smiling. I could tell that we were kindred spirits. Kyshawna was one of the few people to include me in her life, from things as simple as housing resources, programs, conferences and even just hanging out. She was and still is a very intentional and inclusive person on purpose.

She is fairly young compared to me but very powerful, sweet and considerate. Her mentality at such a young age is so breathtaking and inspiring. The way she views herself and her future self is and will be rewarding for so many lives that she will touch as she continues to grow and develop into a young woman.

Kyshawna also has encouraged me to continue to be myself, unapologetically bold, loyal, honest and supportive, even when it's not always reciprocated. Unknowingly, she has even helped stir up a gift that has been lying dormant on the inside of me: Singing. I am forever grateful for the love that she has extended to me and her acceptance of me in her life as one of her Big Sisters. I LOVE YOU, SIS!

Alisa Brooks

I met Kyshawna in a public relations course we took in college. I never thought about the impact we would make in each other's lives. But throughout our time in college, we often helped each other, whether it was with assignments, study habits or just positive motivation to take note of in life.

I was quick to admire how Kyshawna carried herself. When she sets a goal, she does any and everything in her power to make sure it happens. She understands the importance of gratitude and having faith for what's to come. Kyshawna also has one of the biggest hearts I have ever seen. She's always wanting to make sure the people around her are doing just as good. Her initiative to keep growing gets stronger with each passing day.

Kianna Torres

I met Kyshawna six years ago. We were both working at a restaurant trying to pay for college. Being able to watch her grow was something that really inspired me. She was going through a difficult time when I met her, but you would have never known by looking at her. She never spoke down upon herself and never doubted that she would become successful. She spoke only affirmations and had, and continues to have, high standards for herself. Seeing how much she has accomplished with so many odds against her is something special.

There are many who want more for themselves but are afraid to take the risk. She is not one of those people. She is someone who will bet on herself and will continue to do so because she truly believes in herself. I truly see her as an inspiration because there were many times she could have given up, but she didn't. She continues to work hard with all the talents she was given.

There are more and more women that young girls can look up to, and she is definitely one of them. Although you might go through some hardships, she shows you that you can always overcome them while always staying true yourself.

FOR MORE INFORMATION

Please visit www.kyshawnajohnson.com

Made in the USA
Monee, IL
14 November 2023

46449720R00102